E. P. Veerasawmy's *Indian Cookery* is a veritable classic. Dealing with the whole range of recipes from the Indian subcontinent, this book is clearly and succinctly written, with a host of helpful tips for the Western beginner.

D1375426

E. P. VEERASAWMY

Indian Cookery

GRAFTON BOOKS

A Division of the Collins Publishing Group

LONDON GLASGOW
TORONTO SYDNEY AUCKLAND

Grafton Books
A Division of the Collins Publishing Group
8 Grafton Street, London W1X 3LA

Published by Grafton Books 1969
Reprinted 1972, 1973, 1975, 1976, 1978 (twice),
1979, 1981, 1982, 1986

First published in Great Britain by
Herbert Joseph Ltd 1936
Published by Arco Publications 1963
Fourth edition 1968

Copyright © Herbert Joseph Ltd 1936

ISBN 0-583-19663-2

Printed and bound in Great Britain by
Cox & Wyman Ltd, Reading

Set in Intertype Times

Contents

	Preface	7
1	Introduction	9
2	Rice	16
3	Pillaus and Birianis	22
4	Korma – Koormah – Quormah	29
5	Kooftahs	35
6	Kababs	41
7	Chicken, Duck and Game Curries	48
8	Mutton, Lamb, Beef and Pork Curries	59
9	Egg, Liver and Tripe Curries	69
10	Dry Curries – Bhoona Ghosht	73
11	Vindaloos	78
12	Fish – Muchlee – Meen	83
13	Prawns	87
14	Molees	92
15	Legumes – Dhalls – Lentils	97
16	Vegetables and Vegetable Curries	105
17	Foogaths	109
18	Sambals	115
19	Fresh Chutneys	120
20	Bhugias	122
21	Pustholes and Samoosas	126
22	Chupatties, Parattas and Rotis Appums	128
23	Soup – Mulligatawny – Shoorva – Russam	133
24	Sundry Dishes	142
25	Brinjals – (Aubergine) – Byngun	157
26	Saioo – Moorkoo	167
27	Meetias, Indian Sweetmeats and other Sweet Dishes	169
	Glossary	183
	Index	187

Preface

INDIAN cookery is not the cookery of a single nationality or of recent civilization. It dates centuries back and is a combination of the cookery of many nationalities. The result is a complicated art dependent on religion, health, customs, taste and climatic conditions. The Westerner does not realize this until he has lived among Indians for the greater part of his life.

The Indian cook does not depend on weights and measures: he uses his judgment and experience instead, so it is a difficult matter for outsiders to follow him. Failures and disappointment are bound to ensue unless you have something to rely upon.

In the following recipes and descriptions of Indian dishes and food customs, I have stressed, and necessarily so, the importance of using the very best ingredients. As most Western countries excel in the quality of their cattle, poultry, vegetables and other food products, the Western housewife has a great advantage over her Eastern sister, even in the making of Indian dishes. It is when she comes to the selection of the Indian ingredients that the utmost care is necessary: unless she uses the same ingredients that are used in India, she cannot expect the same results. Particularly does this matter when using Curry powder, Curry paste, Mulligatawny paste, Kooftah, Koormah, pepper water and Vindaloo mixtures.

For the convenience of the Western races it is advisable to serve Pillaus, rice and similar dishes on flat meat dishes, and the curries, etc., which rank as entrées, on ordinary entrée or vegetable dishes. Curries should always be served in separate dishes and never with rice as a border.

It is best to eat curry and rice with a dessert spoon and fork: a knife should never be used. A well-cooked curry should not need one. At the tables of the Europeans in India, rice is helped more liberally than curry.

E. P. VEERASAWMY

I

Introduction

CURRIES are universally known, and yet outside India how impossible it seems to get a curry made in the proper way. It is a fallacy to suppose that real curries are unobtainable in European countries. This erroneous idea, promulgated especially by those who have been resident in India, with regard to the ingredients used and the methods employed, is largely responsible for the poor imitations dished up as "Indian Curries" by really capable housewives and eminent chefs. I am certain that it is within the capabilities of every cook to make perfect curries, and I can see no reason why in time these delicious dishes should not be regular adjuncts to the fare of ordinary households, not only because of their delicious flavour, but more especially because of their dietetic and economic value.

In India, the various ingredients used in the making of a curry depend largely on the person making the curry, and it is customary, day by day, for such ingredients to be ground separately into a paste with a little water on what is known as a "curry stone." A little of each of these separately ground ingredients is used for making the curry – the proportions are entirely dependent on the taste and judgment of the cook. Weights and measures are seldom used, and the experience thus gained makes them accomplished in the art of curry making.

Bearing this in mind, and knowing how differently the cuisine of the West is carried on, I have worked out practically every recipe in weights and measures familiar to Western housewives, but even so, individual taste must be exercised. In many cases, instead of worrying over the various ingredients, curry powder can be utilized. In my long experience of many years I have used dozens of different curry powders and have come to the conclusion that the Western housewife is not so much to blame as the makers of these so-called Indian curry powders. A genuine Indian curry powder can and does produce a real Indian curry equal to the very finest that can be produced in India. It is, however, necessary that the right curry powder should be used and right methods employed to get this result. Those who speak of "fresh ingredients" being used in India,

know absolutely nothing beyond what their native Indian
servant has told them.

Every ingredient in a genuine Indian curry powder, is identical
to that which is ground on the curry stone every day in Indian
households. Green ginger and, very occasionally, green corianders, are perhaps rather difficult to get, but they are not always
necessary, as will be seen in the various curry recipes.

A really good curry powder that will keep for years, and
always produce a perfect curry, is made up of many different
seeds, roots and spices, well chosen, well proportioned and well
blended, neither too hot or pungent or too vapid and un-
attractive.

Curry acts on the digestive system with the very best results,
for many of its ingredients are carminative in action, apart from
being aromatic and appetizing.

Essential points to remember:

(1) *Any kind of fat* can be used (instead of ghee), such as
   butter, lard, dripping, margarine or any edible oil.

(2) *Garlic.* – If this is objectionable, either reduce the quantity
   or dispense with it altogether.

(3) *Onions.* – The finer the onions are chopped the better, and
   in many cases spring onions are preferable.

(4) The onions and garlic should never be allowed to brown,
   as they will spoil both the appearance and flavour of the
   curry.

(5) *Acidity.* – Limes and tamarinds are generally used, but
   lemon juice or vinegar are equally satisfactory.

(6) The curry powder or curry ingredients, when added to the
   onions and garlic, and before adding any other ingredients,
   should always be lightly fried or broiled for three or four
   minutes on a slow fire to get rid of the peculiar raw
   flavour of the curry powder or curry ingredients. This is
   known as "Bhoon," and is the most important step in the
   art of curry making. In this connection I would emphasize
   the fact that an inferior curry powder, usually adulterated
   with rice flour, would, at this stage, stick to the bottom of
   the pan and burn. Curries should always be cooked slowly
   to extract all the richness and flavour of the curry seeds,
   and they should never be skimmed.

(7) *Instead of cocoanut milk*, cow's milk, either fresh or sour,
   can be utilized for many of the curries.

(8) *On no account* thicken curry with flour. If the gravy is too
   thin, the addition of milk or cocoanut milk or desiccated

cocoanut, or evaporation with the lid of the pan off, will give you the desired result.

(9) *Apples are never used* in Indian curries, neither are sultanas, almonds, etc. The last are only used in Pillaus and Birianis.

(10) There is no need for any special utensils or fuelling, as nearly every one of these dishes can be cooked in ordinary saucepans on gas cookers, electric or other stoves – where the heat can be regulated – even better than in Deckshas and Chatties on the Chulas (earthen fireplaces) of India.

BOGHAR is the blending of the almost cooked contents of one part of the dish in one pan with the almost cooked contents of the rest of the dish in another pan. The combined ingredients are then cooked together until finished.

BHOON means "to broil" and "to fry," for the material so treated may have some fat or oil with it, or it may be dry and devoid of fat of any sort.

DHUM describes a process whereby the material is cooked between two gentle fires, one above and one below. Usually the one below is a wood fire and is drawn should the heat be excessive. The one above is live charcoal.

GHEE is made from butter, either buffalo or cow butter. When properly made it is butter absolutely free from moisture and impurities. When boiling, it is perfectly still and there is no spluttering. For frying purposes, pure ghee is preferable to butter as it does not burn or blacken when used.

In India, ghee as sold in the markets is often adulterated with nut oil and other fats. But the ghee obtained from Brahmins and the ghee made at home is always pure.

If the ghee is to be kept for any length of time, a few peppercorns are added to it. If the ghee becomes rancid, three or four leaves of the Drumstick tree are added to it, and it is then gradually brought to the boil, stood aside for a few minutes and strained through very fine muslin.

OILS: Such oils as Sesame (gingili), mustard oil, cocoanut oil, cotton-seed oil, etc., are commonly used in every household in India, and sometimes almost exclusively used, as ghee is expensive and out of the reach of the ordinary people.

The ordinary fats that are used in Western countries, such as dripping, suet, margarine, etc., are quite out of the question amongst the Hindus, and seldom used by the Mohammedan. Lard, of course, is only used by the Christians.

LIMES: NIMBU: YELLUMSHIKA. This fruit, allied to the lemon, is largely grown and extensively used in the East for its very valuable qualities. Quite apart from its piquant and refreshing acidity when taken as a drink in the shape of lime juice, etc., it is utilized in the pickles, curries and savouries of India, not only on account of its acidity, but also because of its beneficial action on the digestive system. This fact, outside India, is not realized as it should be. The medical profession use the lime to a great extent, and it is frequently recommended by them as a pleasant summer drink.

As an active digestive agent it should be utilized largely. Preparations of the lime in the form of lime pickle, etc., should be an everyday adjunct to those who cannot easily digest foods such as pork, veal, etc., so extensively consumed by the European races.

TAMARIND: MILEE: PULLEE. This fruit is very extensively grown and used in India. Its marked acidity is utilized to the fullest extent in the cuisine of the East. When the fruit is half ripe, fresh chutneys or Sambals are made out of it, and when thoroughly ripe it is utilized in various ways, principally, however, to acidulate the innumerable curries and other dishes of the country.

The Anglo-Indians and Europeans make a jelly or preserve with it and apart from its very acceptable flavour, it is appreciated for its mildly laxative character. Exported Tamarind is obtainable practically everywhere on the Western market. It is usually packed in glass jars, sweetened or unsweetened. For curries and other savoury dishes only the unsweetened tamarind must be used.

COCOANUT: NARRUL: THAINGA. The cocoanut is the product of the cocoanut palm, grown extensively all over the East and used in some shape or form in every part of the world and by every race. Fresh cocoanuts and dry cocoanuts (copra) are on practically every market.

Cocoanut milk is essential in Indian cookery. It can be made from fresh cocoanuts or desiccated cocoanut. When made with fresh cocoanut it is certainly more mellow and richer in creaminess than when made with desiccated cocoanut.

Cocoanut is also prepared in other ways for curries, sweet-meats, etc., either the white part of the kernel of a fresh cocoanut or the copra is ground into a paste on a curry stone or pounded in a mortar.

Generally speaking, it is wiser to use the milk extracted from the cocoanut rather than the cocoanut itself, for cocoanut is so often indigestible.

SOUR CURDS: DHYE: TYRE. Curd, sour or sweet, and in some form or other, is an article of food familiar to many millions.

From Eastern Europe to beyond Mongolia and Tartary, curds are used almost daily; even the Nomadic tribes look upon it as a necessity.

In India it is considered to have a marked influence on the digestive system, and is accordingly eaten by all castes and classes. Quite apart from its utilization in the making of many dishes, it is no uncommon thing to see it eaten by itself, or with rice, sugar, or salt.

PAH-PAHDS OR PUPPADUMS. These are savoury wafer biscuits made in all parts of India and eaten by Hindus and Mahommedans alike. They are very much in favour in English and Anglo-Indian homes. Madras is particularly noted for them, but they are seldom, if ever, made in private houses. The making of Puppadums is a trade in itself. They are exported packed in tins or cartons and may be had from all the leading Stores. Full directions are given on the tins as to their cooking.

I take this opportunity of explaining what a Puppadum really is and how it is made. The most glutinous Dhall in India, known as Odduth, Urad or Ooloonthoo is used for this purpose. The Dhall is ground and sifted into a very, very fine flour, salt is added and then it is blended into a stiff dough with white of egg, beaten up with a little cold water and a small proportion of Pah-Pahd Khar. The dough is kneaded well and pounded with a pestle which is occasionally dipped in oil (olive, gingili or mustard oil). In this manner it is rendered so pliable that four or five balls the size of a large marble are placed one on top of the other with a little oil between them, and rolled out into a flat biscuit the size of a small teaplate. The layers are then separated and dried in the sun before being stored.

The puppadums may be either thin as in Madras, or thick as in Bombay and Bengal. Occasionally they are also to be had in fancy shapes such as scrolls, shells, etc. In parts of India, puppadums are flavoured with black pepper, ground chillies and Assafœtida (Hing).

BOMBAY DUCK OR BOMMALOE MACHEE. This is a fish somewhat the size of an ordinary herring and is caught in immense quantities off the West coast of India, more especially in the neighbourhood of Bombay. The Anglicized name – "Bombay Duck" – is probably due to the fact that the fish skim the surface of the water rather than swim beneath.

Fresh Bombay Duck is eaten locally, prepared in various

ways, but for export and for use in the English and Anglo-Indian homes in India, it is salted and dried in the sun. The fish for this purpose is prepared as follows:

Cut open and cleaned, head and tail removed, plentifully salted and so thoroughly dried that they often appear like chips of wood. For export they are usually packed in tins, and simple directions for cooking them are to be found on the packages.

To Extract Cocoanut Milk

1st Method

1st Milk.

Freshly scraped or grated cocoanut or very finely cut desiccated cocoanut is moistened with just sufficient water to cover it, placed on the fire, brought to the boil and then pressed through a strainer.

2nd Milk.

The squeezed husk with more water is put back on the fire and the process repeated.

2nd Method

1st Milk.

Pour boiling water just sufficient to moisten and cover the grated kernel of a fresh cocoanut or an equal quantity of very finely desiccated cocoanut. Let it stand for 20 minutes and then squeeze the milk out of it.

2nd Milk.

Repeat the process as for the first milk.

N.B. – If equal parts of cow's milk and water are used it will enhance the mellowness and richness of the cocoanut milk. In extracting cocoanut milk use the ordinary potato presser, as it is so much more effective than the Indian method of squeezing it out with the hand.

Cocoanut Paste for Curries

Another way of preparing cocoanut for curries only is by broiling lightly in a frying pan desiccated cocoanut or finely scraped fresh cocoanut with a little finely minced onion and one or two cloves or garlic.

When cool, bottle for use.

Thick Tamarind Pulp

Macerate in cold water ripe tamarinds. Remove all seeds and fibres until you obtain a thick pulp the consistency of a thick purée. Strain through a coarse strainer.

Thin Tamarind Pulp or Water

Is made in the same way, but the consistency is varied according to the requirements of the particular dish it is wanted for, and it is strained through a fine sieve or tammy.

Dhye (Sour Curds)

Bring a pint of milk gradually to blood heat and drop into it a ball of tamarind about the size of a large walnut. Cover the pan and stand in a warm place for 24 hours. You will find it set. Carefully remove the tamarind and mix the curds with another pint of warm milk. Cover the pan closely and stand aside in a warm place for another 24 hours. The curds will then be fit for use and can also be utilized for producing fresh curds.

A sliced lemon can be used instead of the tamarind.

To Cook Puppadums

(1) Bake in a moderate oven until crisp.

(2) Fry in very hot fat on both sides, but the process is very quick. When the fat is hot enough to fry and not sodden, place the puppadum in it. Press it down with a slice for two or three seconds and it will swell and spread out evenly, otherwise it will curl up. Turn rapidly and cook for another two or three seconds. Lift and place it on a kitchen cloth and flatten it out with another cloth. The cloth will absorb the fat, which is so often objectionable.

To Cook Bombay Ducks

(1) Bake in a hot oven until brown and crisp. It will probably curl up if you do not flatten it out when baking.

(2) Fry in very hot fat on both sides and flatten out with a slice to prevent it curling up. Drain thoroughly.

N.B. – The smell of Bombay Ducks when cooking is unpleasant, but it is an extremely attractive appetiser, and a great adjunct to curries.

II

Rice

(Chawal – Thandu – Arachee)

RICE is extremely nutritious and, cooked properly, it is palatable and acceptable to peoples of all nations as a very valuable vegetable. The particular kind of rice ordinarily used by the well-to-do Indians, Anglo-Indians and Europeans is known as Patna rice or, as the native cook in India calls it, "table rice". Patna rice is of various grades and qualities, and may be had either polished or unpolished. The best results will be obtained by using the finest grade of unpolished Patna rice.

Treatment of Rice Before Cooking

All rice, however clean looking, has a certain amount of loose mill starch adhering to it. It must therefore be thoroughly well washed in several lots of cold water. This will ensure whiteness and prevent clogging.

Plain Boiled Rice (Bhat – Choroo)

Set to soak for at least 20 minutes in cold water 450 g (1 lb) of well-washed unpolished Patna rice. Have ready 3.4 l (6 pints) of boiling water in a roomy and absolutely unstained saucepan. Drain the rice in a colander and add it to the boiling water with a dessertspoonful of salt (rice cooked without salt is very insipid). Stir to prevent the rice caking at the bottom of the pan and then let it boil rapidly for 10 to 12 minutes. The rice will now be sufficiently cooked, and soft enough for a grain to be lightly crushed between the finger and thumb. Now pour the whole contents of the pan into a well-perforated colander (not a sieve) and pour rather less than half a teacupful of cold water over the rice to separate the grains. Drain thoroughly well, and, using a spoon, lift the rice lightly and dish. Rice cooked in this manner will not need heating up or drying in any way.

Rice Cooked by Absorption

Well-washed unpolished Patna rice is set to soak in cold water for at least an hour, it is then drained, a little salt added, and placed in a sauté pan with a close-fitting lid. Boiling water, sufficient to cover and an inch or two over the rice is added. The pan is covered closely and placed on a slow fire until all the water is absorbed and the rice cooked.

Spicy Cocoanut Rice (Copra Kana)

Using a deep *sauté* pan with a close-fitting lid, put into it 113 g (¼ lb) of ghee or butter, 2 tablespoonfuls of finely chopped onion, and a clove or two of garlic, also very finely chopped; 10 whole cardamoms; 10 whole cloves and one or two sticks of Indian cinnamon each about 50 mm (2 inches) long, and ½ a teaspoonful of allspice (whole). Fry these ingredients until the onions are partially cooked but not browned in the least, then add 450 g (1 lb) of well-washed, well-soaked and well-drained Patna rice, and salt to taste. Stir the mixture carefully and continue to fry for two or three minutes longer.

Now pour over the rice sufficient boiling cocoanut milk to cover the rice and stand over it about 40 mm (1½ inches). If short of cocoanut milk add boiling water. Cover the pan closely and cook on a slow fire, stirring occasionally and carefully, until the moisture is entirely absorbed and the rice cooked. This is a most difficult dish to handle, as the cocoanut milk has a tendency to make the grains of rice clog together and stick to the bottom of the pan.

Cocoanut rice is sometimes very pale yellow in colour. This can be achieved by adding ½ a teaspoonful of ground turmeric when frying the onions and spices and before the rice is added.

Simple Cocoanut Rice (Copra Kana)

450 g (1 lb) of well washed, well soaked and well drained Patna rice.

1.1 l (2 pints) of cocoanut milk.

113 g (¼ lb) of ghee or butter.

2 tablespoonfuls of chopped onions.

Salt to taste.

Lightly fry the onions in the ghee or butter, add the rice, salt to taste, cocoanut milk and sufficient boiling water to cover the rice and stand about 25 mm (1 inch) over it. Mix, cover the pan closely and cook on a slow fire stirring lightly and occasionally (to prevent the rice sticking to the bottom of the pan) until the rice is thoroughly cooked and the liquid absorbed. The grains of rice will not be separate owing to the cocoanut milk. Cocoanut rice is usually served with chicken or dry curries and freshly prepared chutneys and sambals.

Cocoanut Milk for Cocoanut Rice

Grate the inner white of the kernel of a large fresh cocoanut or use 8 tablespoonfuls of finely desiccated cocoanut (copra). Place in a saucepan and cover it with 1.1 l (2 pints) of water. Bring to the boil and then let it stand aside for 10 or 15 minutes. Squeeze the liquid out of the cocoanut with an ordinary potato presser. The milk thus extracted can then be used.

Savoury or Yellow Rice

Using a deep sauté pan with a close-fitting lid, lightly fry for about 5 minutes in 113 g (¼ lb) of ghee or butter, 2 tablespoonfuls of chopped onion, a small saltspoonful of finely chopped garlic and two ordinary cloves. Add a teaspoonful of ground turmeric and a saltspoonful of ground cummin seed, cook for another minute or two and then add 450 g (1 lb) of well washed, well soaked and well drained Patna rice and salt to taste. Stir and cook for another 5 minutes. Now add boiling water sufficient to cover the rice and stand over it about 25 or 50 mm (1 or 2 inches). Cover the pan closely and cook on a slow fire until the water is absorbed and the rice cooked.

Do not stir the rice into a pulp, but occasionally lift it lightly with a shallow spoon and toss it over and over until you are sure that every grain is cooked.

Savoury Rice or Cold Cooked Rice

For 450 g (1 lb) of rice put 56g (2 oz) or more of ghee or butter into a saucepan together with a large onion and 2 cloves of garlic minced finely, also 6 whole cloves, 6 or 8 cardamoms and a 50 mm (2 inch) stick of cinnamon. Fry these ingredients until the onion is cooked, but not browned.

Toss the rice into the mixture, mix lightly, salt to taste, and, when the rice is warmed through, serve garnished with slices of hard boiled eggs and cripsly fried onions.

Rice and Spaghetti (*Bhat Aur Savia*)

(An Anglo-Indian dish)

450 g (1 lb) of well washed, well soaked and drained Patna rice.

113 g ($\frac{1}{4}$ lb) of spaghetti in 50 mm (2 inch) lengths.

113 g ($\frac{1}{4}$ lb) of ghee or 170 g (6 ozs) of butter.

1 large onion, preferably Spanish, chopped finely.

$\frac{1}{2}$ teaspoonful of finely chopped garlic.

6 or 8 whole cloves.

A piece of cinnamon, 50 mm (2 inches) long.

$\frac{1}{2}$ teaspoonful of cummin seed.

$\frac{1}{2}$ teaspoonful of allspice (whole).

Salt to taste.

Cook the onions, garlic and spices in the ghee or butter, but do not brown the onions. Now fry for 2 or 3 minutes in this mixture the rice and spaghetti. Salt to taste. Add boiling water sufficient to cover and stand over the rice about 40 mm ($1\frac{1}{2}$ inches) or more. Cover the pan closely and cook on a slow fire until all moisture is absorbed and the rice is cooked. Lightly stir occasionally to prevent the rice sticking to the bottom of the pan.

Kitcheree

450 g (1 lb) of Patna rice.

113 g ($\frac{1}{4}$ lb) of Moong Dhall or Egyptian lentils.

> Mix together and wash thoroughly in cold water and let it soak in fresh cold water for 1 hour or longer.

170 g (6 ozs) of ghee or 225 g ($\frac{1}{2}$ lb) of butter.

2 heaped tablespoonfuls of chopped onions.

$\frac{1}{2}$ teaspoonful of very finely chopped garlic.

10 cloves, 10 whole cardamoms.

2 sticks of cinnamon, each 50 mm (2 inches) long.

$\frac{1}{2}$ teaspoonful of allspice (whole).

6 thin slices of fresh green or pickled ginger.

1 teaspoonful of ground turmeric. Salt.

Use a roomy saucepan with a close-fitting lid and put into it the butter, onions, garlic, spices and ginger. Cook these ingredients but do not let the onions brown. Drain the water thoroughly from the mixture of rice and Dhall and add this mixture to the other ingredients in the pan. Now add the turmeric and salt to taste. Lightly toss the mixture together, using a broad, flat, wooden spoon or spatula, and cook on a very slow fire for 4 or 5 minutes. Now add boiling water sufficient to cover the rice and stand over it about 25 mm (1 inch) or slightly more. Cover the pan closely and cook on a slow fire until the moisture is absorbed and the rice is cooked. Before serving, sprinkle the Kitcheree with about 2 tablespoonfuls of fresh milk. Serve garnished with slices of hard-boiled eggs and rings of crisp fried onions.

Kitcheree (Plain)

    4 parts of rice.
    1 part of Dhall or Egyptian lentils.

Both should be well washed, soaked and drained.

Using a deep sauté pan, place this mixture in it and add boiling water sufficient to cover and stand over it 25 or 50 mm (1 or 2 inches). Salt to taste. Cover the pan closely and cook on a slow fire until the grains of rice are soft and the moisture absorbed. Then gradually add a little oil, ghee or butter, tossing the Kitcheree lightly so that the fat added is evenly distributed.

To Reheat or Warm Up Plain Boiled Rice

The cold cooked rice is added to a saucepan containing boiling water with a very little salt in it, stirred, allowed to come to the boil, then drained, but no cold water is poured over it.

To Utilize Rice Water

The water in which the rice has been boiled is a good basis for white soups and purées. It also makes a pleasant, cooling and effective summer drink, flavoured with sugar and orange or lemon juice.

Savoury Rice for Garnishes or as a Vegetable or an Entrée

Utilizing Cold Cooked Rice:

    (a) In a *sauté* pan and on a slow fire lightly fry in ghee or butter a tablespoonful of chopped or very finely sliced onions. Toss the cold cooked rice in it and slightly flavour with ground white pepper. Let the rice warm thoroughly before serving.

    (b) Vary the above by adding to the onions one or two

skinned and chopped tomatoes or a little tomato purée and grated cheese. – (Anglo-Indian.)

(c) Toss cold cooked rice and a saltspoonful of ground turmeric in the pan in which kidneys, bacon, liver and bacon or sausages have been cooked, and use as a garnish for these dishes. – (Anglo-Indian.)

(d) Cold meats, or poultry of any kind, cut up into small pieces, warmed in the rice and served with chutneys, sambals or Indian pickles, make excellent entrées. – (Anglo-Indian.)

Pillaus and Birianis

(Frequently referred to as Pilaffs, Pulaos, Pillaws)

Of all the delicious, rich and luxurious Moglai dishes from time immemorial, Pillaus and Birianis have held the foremost place in the cuisine of the Orient.

Pillaus and Birianis are usually made with what is known as Pillau rice (various kinds and grades), but as this rice is expensive and seldom obtainable outside India, the finest grade of un-polished Patna rice can be used.

A Pillau is a combination of rice and meat or poultry, etc., cooked in ghee or butter and spices. The ordinary cook in India, however, very seldom has the knowledge or the materials to turn out a real Pillau, and the consequence is that only imitations of this dish are frequently served. The cooking in India is somewhat tedious and complicated, for two separate dishes are partially cooked and then combined, and the cooking finished by a very slow process known as "Dhum", *i.e.*, with a drawn fire under the pan and a live charcoal fire on the lid covering the pan.

With European utensils and fuelling this dish can be produced to perfection provided the instructions here given are carried out.

The author has been able with perfect ease to produce this dish on an ordinary gas cooker and with the ordinary English cooking utensils, to the amazement and entire satisfaction of even princely visitors from India.

Moglai Biriani

Section A – Korma

Two chickens jointed up and marinaded for 2 hours in the following mixture:

570 ml (1 pint) of Solid Dhye (sour curds).
2 heaped tablespoonfuls of chopped onions.

1 teaspoonful of finely chopped fresh or pickled ginger.
½ teaspoonful of finely chopped garlic.
2 tablespoonfuls of ground corianders.
1 heaped teaspoonful of ground turmeric.
½ teaspoonful of ground pepper.
1 dessertspoonful of ground Kus Kus (poppy seeds).
1 dessertspoonful of ground almonds.

In 56 g (2 ozs) or more of ghee or butter, fry lightly for 2 or 3 minutes 1 heaped tablespoonful of finely chopped onions and 1 or 2 cloves of garlic, thinly sliced; 6 to 8 ordinary cloves; 6 to 8 whole cardamoms: two 50 mm (2 inch) sticks of cinnamon.

Add to this the marinaded chicken and the whole of the marinade, and allow the chicken to cook in its own juice without the addition of any stock or water. Mix well, cover the pan closely and cook on a slow fire until the chicken is cooked and tender. Salt to taste.

SECTION B – PILLAU RICE

910 g (2 lb) of Pillau or finest grade of Patna rice, thoroughly well washed in cold water and set to soak for 2 or 4 hours in fresh cold water. Then well drained.

680 g (1½ lb) of ghee or butter.
1 onion and 1 clove of garlic, both chopped finely.
½ teaspoonful of saffron, steeped in ½ a teacupful of warm water.
½ teaspoonful of whole allspice.
10 whole cardamoms.
10 whole cloves.
Two 50 mm (2 inch) sticks of cinnamon.

As this Pillau rice will swell considerably, and the Korma will subsequently be added to it, it is essential that the pan should be sufficiently large and with a close-fitting lid.

Fry in the ghee or butter for 2 or 3 minutes the onions (without browning), garlic and spices, then add the rice and mix it lightly. Continue the frying on a slow fire for 4 or 5 minutes longer. Add the steeped saffron and water, salt to taste, and sufficient boiling water to cover the rice and stand 25 or 50 mm (1 or 2 inches) over it. Cover the pan closely and cook on a very slow fire until the rice has absorbed all the water and is thoroughly cooked.

It will be necessary to watch the cooking of the rice very carefully, occasionally using a slice or spatula to toss it over and over,

rather than mix it. This will ensure every grain being cooked
and avoid pulping, for when thoroughly cooked each grain
should be separate.

When the rice is nearly cooked, work into it:

225 g (½ lb) of sultanas (Kismis), 113 g (¼ lb) of blanched almonds (Badam), 113 g (¼ lb) of blanched pistachios (Pis-
tach), fried lightly in ghee or butter, and toss into it 450 g
(1 lb) of dried Kajoors (Perisna dates).

SECTION C – THE FINISH

This is a blending of the Korma with the rice, and must be
carefully done to prevent the breaking up of the meat and the
pulping of the rice.

Take each piece of the chicken and work it carefully into the
rice, using up as much of the gravy as possible. Cover the pan
very closely to prevent the aroma escaping and stand it on a
very, very slow fire. In India, the fire is drawn and only hot ashes
and embers are left under it, and on the lid is placed a gentle
heat in the shape of a little live charcoal.

The Biriani can be made very much richer by increasing the
amount of ghee. When Pillau rice is used it is not unusual to
have equal weights of rice and ghee.

This Biriani is served piled up on gold or silver salvers, and
garnished with pure gold or silver leaf.

Rice for Pillau

450 g (1 lb) of Patna rice well washed in cold water and set to
soak in cold water for 2 hours or longer, then thoroughly
drained; 225 g (½ lb) of butter or ghee; 1 large onion and 2
cloves of garlic, chopped; ½ teaspoonful of saffron (steeped in
half a teacupful of warm water); 12 cloves; 12 whole cardamoms; 2 sticks of cinnamon, each about 50 mm (2 inches)
long, and ½ teaspoonful of allspice (whole), 113 g (4 ozs) of
sultanas and 56 g (2 ozs) of blanched almonds (lightly fried
in butter).

Use a deep *sauté* pan with a close-fitting lid. Fry in the butter
or ghee the onions (but do not brown), garlic and spices, then
add the rice and, tossing it lightly, continue the frying on a slow
fire for 4 or 5 minutes longer. Add the steeped saffron and water,
salt to taste and sufficient boiling water to cover the rice and stand
25 or 50 mm (1 or 2 inches) over it. Cover the pan closely, and

cook on a very slow fire until the rice has absorbed all the water and is thoroughly cooked – each grain should be separate. Finally mix lightly into the rice the fried sultanas and almonds.

Moorgee Kabab Pillau

(1) A plump chicken trussed as for roasting but with the legs scored.
(2) Rice for Pillau (see page 24).
(3) A Korma mixture made of:

1 teaspoonful of ground turmeric, 1 dessertspoonful of ground coriander, $\frac{1}{2}$ teaspoonful of ground black pepper, 1 dessertspoonful of ground Kus Kus, 1 dessertspoonful of ground almonds, a teacupful of Dhye (sour curds). Salt to taste.

Fill the bird lightly with some of the Pillau rice and rub well into it a little of the above mixture. Then braise it in a little ghee or butter to which has been added a tablespoonful of finely chopped onions and a clove of garlic very finely sliced.

After 10 minutes' braising, pour the rest of the mixture over the bird and continue the cooking, basting it every now and again until cooked. Untruss the bird and dish it on a bed of Pillau rice and pour over it the gravy.

Small birds such as snipe (Chaha), quail (Buteer), wild duck (Moorghabe), partridge (Burra Buteer), teal (Teetur), pigeon (Kaboothar), etc., are often cooked in this delicious manner.

Kooftah Pillau

Blend:

450g (1 lb) of finely minced mutton or beef with a table-spoonful of finely chopped onions.
$\frac{1}{2}$ teaspoonful of chopped garlic.
1 heaped dessertspoonful of Kooftah mixture.
1 tablespoonful of flour.
1 egg.
Salt to taste.

Form into balls the size of large walnuts, and fry in ghee or other fat.

Prepare the rice for Pillau (see page 24) and blend the Kooftahs in it. Cover the pan to keep the aroma in until required.

Prawn Pillau

Fry lightly for 3 or 4 minutes 1 tablespoonful of chopped onions in 56 g (2 ozs) of ghee or other fat. Add to it a dessert-spoonful of Korma mixture. Cook for 3 or 4 minutes longer.

Add a teacupful of Dhye (solid, sour curds) and as many cooked prawns as desired. Simmer for 5 minutes. Salt to taste, then blend this Prawn Korma with the Pillau rice. (See page 24).

Cover the pan to keep in the aroma until ready to be served.

Madras Prawn Pillau

450 g (1 lb) of well washed, soaked and drained Patna rice, 113 g (4 ozs) of ghee or butter, 1 tablespoonful of chopped onion, ½ teaspoonful of chopped garlic, 6 cardamoms, 6 cloves, two 50 mm (2 inch) sticks of cinnamon, ½ teaspoonful of ground turmeric.

Fry lightly in the ghee or butter for 3 or 4 minutes, the onions, garlic, spices and turmeric. Then add the rice and continue the slow frying for a further 3 or 4 minutes. Now add sufficient boiling cocoanut milk to cover the rice and stand over it an inch to one and a half inches. Cover the pan closely and continue the cooking on a slow fire until the cocoanut milk is absorbed and the rice cooked. Then envelope in it sufficient cooked prawns that have been previously tossed in ghee with a sprinkling of ground black pepper and ground chillies. Serve garnished with crisp fried onions.

Deccan Mutton or Lamb Pillau

Prepare the rice for this Pillau as on page 24. The Korma to blend with it is made with thick slices of lamb or mutton as described on page 24. The Korma and Pillau rice are then carefully blended together.

Cover the pan to keep the aroma in until wanted.

Madras Mutton or Lamb Pillau

910 g (2 lb) of lamb or mutton cutlets or 12 mm (½ inch) thick slices of lamb or mutton, boiled, in sufficient water to cover them, until tender.

In 113 g (4 ozs) of ghee or butter, fry lightly for 3 or 4 minutes:
4 tablespoonfuls of chopped onions, ½ teaspoonful of chopped garlic, one 50 mm (2 inch) stick of cinnamon, 6 cardamoms, 6 cloves, ½ teaspoonful of chopped green ginger.

Stir into it 450 g (1 lb) of well washed, soaked and drained Patna rice and, mixing all together, continue the slow frying for another 4 or 5 minutes. Then pour over it the boiling stock in which the mutton has been cooked, sufficient to cover and stand over the rice about 25 to 40 mm (1 to 1½ inches). If insufficient stock, add boiling water. Salt to taste. Cover the pan closely and cook until the water is absorbed and the rice cooked.

Then envelope in it the cooked meat and 56 g (2 ozs) of blanched almonds and sultanas which have been previously lightly fried in ghee or butter. Dish and garnish with crisply fried onions.

Madras Chicken Pillau

> 1 fowl boiled till tender in just sufficient water to cover it, with 3 or 4 shallots to flavour the stock.
> 450 g (1 lb) of well washed, soaked and drained Patna rice.
> 113 g (4 ozs) of ghee or butter.
> 6 cardamoms.
> 6 cloves.
> One 50 mm (2 inch) stick of cinnamon.

Fry in the ghee the spices and rice for about 5 minutes, stirring all the time. Add to it sufficient of the chicken stock to cover the rice and stand 25 or 50 mm (1 or 2 inches) over it. If the stock is insufficient, add boiling water. Salt to taste. Simmer on a slow fire until the water is absorbed and the rice cooked. Then stir into it 113 g (4 ozs) of sultanas and 56 g (2 ozs) of blanched almonds, slit in halves.

To Serve:

A layer of the Pillau rice is placed on a flat dish on which the fowl, either whole or jointed, is placed, then covered with the remainder of the rice and garnished with hard-boiled eggs cut in quarters and crisp fried onions.

Vegetable Pillau

For this dish it will be necessary to have about a pint of macédoine of cooked vegetables such as peas, carrots, and beans, etc., drained thoroughly; 450 g (1 lb) of Patna or Pillau rice, thoroughly well washed and set to soak in cold water for an hour or two and then well drained.

Use a *sauté* pan and put into it:

113 g ($\frac{1}{4}$ lb) of butter or ghee, an onion or two very finely sliced, 2 cloves of garlic chopped up finely, 8 ordinary cloves, 1 stick of cinnamon 50 mm (2 inches) long, 8 whole cardamoms, $\frac{1}{2}$ teaspoonful of allspice (whole), $\frac{1}{2}$ teaspoonful of ground turmeric.

Fry these ingredients but do not let them brown. Now add the rice to the onions and spices. Stir the whole lightly and cook for about 4 or 5 minutes. Then pour over the rice boiling water sufficient to cover and stand over it about 25 mm (1 inch) or more. Add salt to taste, cover the pan closely and cook on a slow fire until the rice is cooked and the moisture absorbed. If the moisture has not been sufficiently absorbed remove the lid of the pan and this will help considerably.

Now lightly mix the vegetables into the rice, and, if liked, 56 g (2 ozs) of sultanas and 56 g (2 ozs) of blanched almonds or other nuts, which have been lightly fried in ghee or butter.

IV

Korma—Koormah—Quormah

THE dishes under one or other of these designations are invariably Moglai or Mahommedan. They are rich and spicy but not hot: usually served with Pillau, Kitcheree or Cocoanut Rice.

With few exceptions the meat used is marinaded in a mixture in which the chief ingredient is Dhye (sour curds), known as Tyre in Southern India.

Duck Korma (Budduck Ka Korma)

Marinade for an hour or two a duck cut up into convenient pieces in a mixture of a teacupful of sour curds (Dhye) and:

1 tablespoonful of ground corianders.
1 dessertspoonful of ground almonds.
1 teaspoonful of ground turmeric.
½ teaspoonful of ground cummin seed.
A generous pinch of ground chillies.
A generous pinch of ground black pepper.

In a tablespoonful of ghee or other fat, fry lightly a sliced onion, 2 or 3 slices of garlic, 2 or 3 cloves, 2 or 3 cardamoms and a 50 mm (2 inch) stick of cinnamon. To this add the duck and the marinade. Mix well, cover the pan, and cook slowly until the duck is tender. Salt and lemon juice to taste.

Duck Korma (Budduck Ka Korma)

(Another way)

One duck cut up into convenient pieces and marinaded for an hour or two in a marinade made with a teacupful of sour curds and 2 heaped tablespoonfuls of Korma mixture.

In 56 g (2 ozs) of ghee or other fat fry lightly:

1 onion and 1 clove of garlic both finely sliced.
3 or 4 cloves.

3 or 4 cardamoms.
1 50 mm (2 inch) stick of cinnamon.

Add the duck and the marinade. Mix thoroughly, cover the pan and simmer until the meat is tender. Add salt and lemon juice to taste.

Chicken Korma (*Moorgee Korma*)

Joint up a fair-sized chicken and marinade it for an hour in a mixture of two or three tablespoonfuls of Dhye (sour curds), a heaped teaspoonful of ground turmeric, 1 clove of garlic, either ground into a paste or finely minced.

Using a stew pan, put in:

56 g (2 ozs) or more of ghee or other fat.
1 large onion halved and sliced down finely.
1 clove of garlic finely sliced lengthwise.
25 mm (1 inch) pieces of fresh or pickled ginger finely sliced.
6 whole cloves.
6 whole cardamoms.
A stick of cinnamon about 50 mm (2 inches) long.

Cook until the onions are half cooked, then add one heaped tablespoonful of Korma mixture. Stir well and cook on a slow fire for 3 or 4 minutes longer.

Now add the chicken and marinade. Mix lightly but thoroughly. Cover the pan closely and simmer until the chicken is done. Do not add liquid of any sort; the Korma will form a gravy of its own, thick and rich. Salt and lemon juice to taste.

Chicken Korma (*Moorgee Korma*)

(Another way)

Marinade for an hour or two a jointed chicken in a mixture of:

285 ml (½ pint) of curds.
1 tablespoonful of ground corianders.
1 tablespoonful of finely desiccated or freshly scraped cocoanut.
Rather less than 1 teaspoonful of ground turmeric.
½ teaspoonful of ground cummin seed.
½ teaspoonful of ground chillies
1 dessertspoonful of ground almonds.

Fry lightly in 56 g (2 ozs) of ghee or other fat, 2 tablespoonfuls of chopped onions and 1 or 2 cloves of garlic, sliced finely.

Add the chicken and the whole of the marinade. Mix well and simmer until the chicken is sufficiently done. Add salt and lemon juice.

Chicken Korma (*Moorgee Ka Korma*)

(Another way)

1 chicken, jointed.
1 small onion and 2 cloves of garlic, finely sliced.
4 cardamoms.
4 cloves.
A 50 mm (2 inch) stick of cinnamon.
2 tablespoonfuls of Korma mixture.
285 ml ($\frac{1}{2}$ pint) of sour curds (Dhye).
56 g (2 ozs) of ghee or other fat.
1 tablespoonful of desiccated cocoanut.

Fry lightly in the ghee or other fat for 2 or 3 minutes the onions, garlic, cloves, cardamoms and cinnamon. Then add the Korma mixture, the Dhye and the jointed chicken. Cover the pan closely and simmer the contents for 10 minutes. Now add sufficient water to form a thickish gravy and continue the cooking with the pan covered until the chicken is tender.

Five minutes before serving add the cocoanut, either freshly scraped or finely desiccated. Salt and lemon juice to taste.

Chicken Korma (*Moorgee Ka Korma*)

(Another way)

One chicken jointed and marinaded for an hour or two in:

2 teacupfuls of Dhye or sour curds, blended with: 1 dessertspoonful of Korma mixture; 1 tablespoonful of finely chopped onions; 1 or more cloves of garlic, finely sliced; a piece of fresh or pickled ginger 12 mm ($\frac{1}{2}$ inch) long, chopped finely.

Warm 56 g (2 ozs) of ghee or butter in a sauté pan and add to it:

A clove of garlic, finely sliced; 1 tablespoonful of chopped onions; 4 cloves; 4 whole cardamoms; a 50 mm (2 inch) stick of cinnamon.

Cook over a slow fire – don't let the onions brown – and add the chicken and marinade. Mix, cover the pan closely and simmer until the chicken is tender. Salt and lemon juice to taste.

This curry cooks in the Dhye and needs no other liquor.

Chicken Korma (for Pillau) –
Moorgee Ka Korma

1 chicken, 1.4 to 1.8 kg (3 to 4 lb), jointed into convenient sizes.
2 tablespoonfuls of chopped onions.
½ teaspoonful of chopped garlic.
½ teaspoonful of fresh or pickled green ginger.
1 teaspoonful of ground Kus Kus (poppy seeds).
10 cloves.
10 whole cardamoms.
1 50 mm (2 inch) stick of cinnamon.
¼ teaspoonful of ground allspice.
1 dessertspoonful of Korma mixture.
2 teacupfuls of sour curds (solid).
56 g (2 ozs) of ghee.
½ teaspoonful of peppercorns.

Warm the ghee and add to it all the above ingredients, except the chicken, Korma mixture and Dhye. Cook on a slow fire for 4 or 5 minutes, then add the Korma mixture. Mix and continue the cooking for another 3 or 4 minutes. Add the jointed chicken and curds.

Mix well, cover the pan *closely*, and simmer until the chicken is tender. Salt and lemon juice to taste. On no account add any water or stock. There will be quite sufficient gravy in it.

Mutton Korma (Ghosht Ka Korma)

450 g (1 lb) of fresh mutton, cut up into pieces about 40 mm (1½ inches) square, and 12 mm (½ inch) thick.
2 or more tablespoonfuls of ghee or butter.
2 heaped tablespoonfuls of chopped onions.
½ teaspoonful of chopped garlic.
1 teaspoonful of chopped fresh or pickled ginger.
Spices: 4 cloves, 6 cardamoms, stick of cinnamon 50 mm (2 inches) in length.
1 heaped tablespoonful of Korma mixture.

2 tablespoonfuls of Dhye (sour curds).
1 tablespoonful of finely cut desiccated cocoanut (copra).
Salt.

Use a stewpan and put into it the ghee or butter, onions, garlic, ginger and spices and cook until onions are on the verge of browning, but do not brown them. Now add the Korma mixture, stir well and continue the cooking for another 2 or 3 minutes, then add the meat and Dhye.

Cover the pan and simmer the contents on a slow fire – watching carefully to see that it does not burn – until the meat is tender. Finally add the cocoanut and salt to taste. A squeeze of lemon juice will make an improvement.

Korma of Lamb or Mutton (Ghosht Ka Korma)

450 g (1 lb) of lamb or mutton cut up in rather large pieces.
56 g (2 ozs) of butter or ghee.
2 heaped tablespoonfuls of chopped onions.
½ teaspoonful of finely sliced garlic.
1 teaspoonful of finely sliced green giner.
6 cloves, 6 cardamoms and a stick of cinnamon about 50 or
    75 mm (2 or 3 inches) long.
1 heaped tablespoonful of Korma mixture.
1 heaped tablespoonful of ground almonds.
1 teacupful of Dhye (sour curds).
1 tablespoonful of finely cut desiccated cocoanut or 285 ml
    (½ pint) of thick cocoanut milk.
Salt.

Cook the onions, garlic, ginger and spices in the butter or ghee until the onions are cooked, but not browned. Add the Korma mixture. Stir well and continue the cooking on a slow fire for 4 or 5 minutes.

Then add the meat, Dhye and ground almonds, cover the pan closely and cook slowly until the meat is tender. Then add the cocoanut and salt to taste.

Mutton or Lamb Korma (Ghosht Ka Korma)

Trimmed mutton or lamb cutlets are usually used. They are marinaded for an hour or longer in a mixture made up as follows:
For 910 g (2 lb) of cutlets use:

2 tablespoonfuls of Dhye, Tyre or sour curds
1 teaspoonful of ground turmeric.
½ teaspoonful of ground cummin seed.
1 clove of garlic finely chopped.

Use a roomy saucepan, put into it 113 g (¼ lb) of ghee or other fat:

1 large onion, finely chopped.
1 clove of garlic, sliced lengthwise.
A piece of fresh or pickled green ginger about 25 mm (1 inch) long, chopped finely or pounded into a paste.
6 whole cloves.
6 whole cardamoms.
1 50 mm (2 inch) stick of whole cinnamon.

Cook until the onions are fairly well cooked but not browned. Then add 2 heaped tablespoonfuls of Korma mixture and, stirring the mixture thoroughly, cook it on a slow fire for 4 or 5 minutes.

Now add the marinaded meat and all the marinade. Mix the whole lightly and yet thoroughly, and, covering the pan closely, simmer on a slow fire until the meat is tender. Add salt to taste and a squeeze of lemon juice.

The Korma will form its own gravy, which will be thick and rich, but should it need moisture whilst cooking, add either stock or water just sufficient to form the gravy.

Korma Curry

Add 450 g (1 lb) of beef or mutton cut up into convenient sizes to a mixture of:

285 ml (½ pint) of sour curds.
1 onion and 2 cloves of garlic, finely chopped.
½ teaspoonful of ground pepper.
½ teaspoonful of ground ginger.
½ teaspoonful of ground cummin seed.
½ teaspoonful of ground chillies
½ teaspoonful of ground mustard seed.

Fry lightly a sliced onion in 1 tablespoonful of ghee or other fat. Add the mixture of meat and spices and cook slowly until the meat is tender. Salt and a squeeze of lemon juice is added before serving. If possible, cook this curry without water or stock. The curds will help to form a thick rich gravy if slowly cooked.

V

Kooftahs

KOOFTAHS are largely favoured throughout India, but more specially in the Deccan and Central India. They are usually balls of minced mutton or beef, blended with onions, garlic, ginger and certain spices, and cooked in a curry sauce which is made to taste and varies according to the locality. Prawns, fish, etc., are also converted into Kooftah curries.

It is very essential that these curries should be carefully handled. especially when stirring, as the balls of meat are apt to clog together or break up. It is advisable, therefore, to shake the pan gently now and again rather than to stir the curry.

Kooftah Curry

450 g (1 lb) of fresh meat very finely minced or pounded.

1 small onion ⎫
1 clove of garlic ⎭ finely minced.

A small pinch of pepper, ground cinnamon, ground cloves, ground cardamoms.

Blend these ingredients together with an egg. Salt to taste.

With slightly floured hands form into balls the size of a large walnut. Fry these light brown in boiling ghee or other fat and drain. Then using some of the fat, fry in it a large onion and 2 cloves of garlic, finely sliced, and add to it:

1 tablespoonful of ground corianders.
1 teaspoonful of ground turmeric.
½ teaspoonful of ground mustard seed.
½ teaspoonful of ground cummin seed.
½ teaspoonful of ground ginger.
½ teaspoonful of ground chillies.

Lightly cook these ingredients for 3 or 4 minutes, then add a pint of thin cocoanut milk. Salt to taste and a squeeze of lemon juice.

Add the balls of meat and simmer gently for about half an hour. Shake the pan occasionally, but do not stir it as the balls of meat may break up.

Madras Kooftah Curry

450 g (1 lb) of finely minced fresh lean beef or mutton blended with:
2 or 3 fresh or pickled chillies (finely chopped).
1 heaped teaspoonful of Kooftah mixture.
1 tablespoonful of chopped onions.
1 clove of garlic, very finely minced.
1 teaspoonful of flour.
1 egg.
Salt to taste.

With slightly floured hands form the mixture into balls the size of a large walnut.

Fry lightly in a stewpan for 3 or 4 minutes in 56 g (2 ozs) of ghee or other fat:

1 tablespoonful of chopped onion.
1 clove of garlic finely minced.
2 dry red chillies, cut lengthwise in halves and the inner seed removed,

and now add to it:

1 tablespoonful of curry paste.
1 teaspoonful of Kooftah mixture.

Stir thoroughly and cook gently for a few minutes longer. Then add gradually thin cocoanut milk sufficient to form a thickish gravy and a dessertspoonful of tamarind pulp. Salt to taste. Bring to the boil, drop the balls of meat in, one by one, and cook slowly with the pan uncovered for about half an hour, when the meat should be thoroughly cooked.

This curry should not be stirred, or the balls of meat will break up. Just shake the pan every now and again.

Deccan Kooftah Curry

450 g (1 lb) of finely minced fresh lean beef or mutton mixed with:
1 dessertspoonful of finely chopped onions.

1 heaped teaspoonful of Kooftah mixture.
Salt to taste.
1 teaspoonful of flour.
1 egg.

With slightly floured hands form the mixture into balls the size of a large walnut.

In a stewpan fry lightly for 3 or 4 minutes in 56 g (2 ozs) of ghee or other fat:

1 tablespoonful of chopped onion.
1 clove of garlic, finely sliced.
2 whole cardamoms.
2 cloves.
A 50 mm (2 inch) stick of cinnamon.

Add to it:

1 dessertspoonful of curry powder.
1 teaspoonful of Kooftah mixture.

Stir thoroughly, cook for 3 or 4 minutes longer, then add either 2 fresh tomatoes, finely chopped, or a dessertspoonful of tomato paste: Now add gradually, water or stock sufficient to form a thick gravy. Bring to the boil, add salt to taste, and then drop in, one by one, the balls of meat. Cover the pan and simmer for about half an hour, when the meat should be thoroughly cooked.

Be careful not to stir this curry after the balls of meat have been added, or they will pulp. Just shake the pan every now and again. 2 tablespoonfuls of thick cocoanut milk, added at the last, will improve this curry.

Prawn Kooftah Curry

1 large tin or bottle of prawns, finely minced and blended with:
1 dessertspoonful of finely chopped onion.
1 or 2 fresh pickled chillies (chopped).
1 dessertspoonful of flour.
1 teaspoonful of Kooftah mixture.
1 egg.

With floured hands form this mixture into firm round balls the size of large walnuts.

In 56 g (2 ozs) of ghee or other fat, fry lightly for a few minutes without browning:

> 1 finely chopped onion.
> 1 minced clove of garlic.

Add to it:

> 1 teaspoonful of Kooftah mixture and
> 1 heaped dessertspoonful of curry paste.

Mix and continue the cooking for another 2 or 3 minutes. Convert this into a thickish gravy by adding gradually to it thin cocoanut milk or ordinary cow's milk. Bring to the boil. Salt and lemon juice to taste. Simmer for 10 or 15 minutes, then drop the balls in. Cook for at least 10 minutes longer with the pan uncovered. After adding the balls, do not stir this curry, but shake the pan occasionally. Lobster meat or almost any kind of cooked fish can be utilized in the same way.

Prawn Kooftah Curry

(Another way)

Prawn Mixture.

> 18 prawns.
> 1 small onion }
> 1 clove of garlic } minced finely.
> 1 teaspoonful of ground corianders.
> ½ teaspoonful of ground turmeric.
> ½ teaspoonful of ground cummin seed.
> ½ teaspoonful of ground mustard seed.

Pound these ingredients with enough eggs and a little flour to make a paste which can be formed with floured hands into balls the size of a large walnut.

Curry Mixture.

> 1 onion and }
> 2 cloves of garlic } sliced finely.
> 1 dessertspoonful of ground corianders.
> 1 teaspoonful of ground turmeric.
> ½ teaspoonful of ground cummin seed.
> ½ teaspoonful of ground mustard seed.
> ½ teaspoonful of ground ginger.
> ½ teaspoonful of ground chillies.

2 ordinary cloves.
2 cardamoms.
1 stick of cinnamon about 50 mm (2 inches) long.
6 peppercorns.
2 tablespoonfuls of ghee.
Salt to taste.
Thin cocoanut milk.

Fry lightly the onions and garlic in the ghee, then add all the other curry ingredients, except the cocoanut milk. Stir lightly and fry for 5 minutes on a slow fire. Then add sufficient cocoanut milk to form a fairly thick sauce. Bring slowly to the boil, add the balls of prawn mixture and simmer gently for 15 minutes. Salt and lemon juice to taste.

This curry must be carefully handled, as the balls are likely to pulp.

Cold Meat Kooftah Curry

450 g (1 lb) of finely minced lean cold meat of any kind blended with:

1 dessertspoonful of Kooftah mixture.
1 tablespoonful of finely chopped onions.
1 tablespoonful of flour.
Salt to taste.
1 egg.

With floured hands make into balls the size of a large walnut. Fry lightly for 3 or 4 minutes in 56 g (2 ozs) of ghee or other fat:

1 tablespoonful of chopped onion.
2 cloves of garlic, chopped finely.

Then add: 1 tablespoonful of curry powder and 1 dessert-spoonful of tomato paste. Mix well and continue the slow cooking for 3 or 4 minutes longer, and, gradually adding water, convert it into a fairly thick gravy. Salt and lemon juice to taste. Then drop the balls of meat into it, one by one, and simmer for 10 minutes.

Anglo-Goanese Kooftah Curry

Fry lightly in 28 g (1 oz) of ghee or other fat for 3 or 4 minutes:

1 onion
2 cloves of garlic } chopped finely.

2 or 3 fresh or pickled chillies, cut lengthwise in halves. Mix into this a dessertspoonful of curry powder and a teaspoonful of tomato paste, and continue the slow cooking for another 2 or 3 minutes. Then, with a little water, convert this into a thickish gravy. Salt and lemon juice to taste. Bring to the boil, and then simmer.

Take 450 g (1 lb) of sausage meat and, with slightly floured hands, make into small balls the size of large marbles and drop them, one by one, into the simmering sauce.

Do not stir, but shake the pan gently now and again to prevent the balls from caking together.

VI

Kababs

In all Islamic countries Kababs of various kinds are prepared as an every-day dish, and it is quite a familiar sight to see Kababs being roasted before charcoal fires in the bazaars of the Orient and sold with Rotis of different kinds. Kababs differ in different parts, both in appearance and flavour, and also in materials. The further East we go the more spicy Kababs become, and their formation is very considerably altered.

They may be made of large pieces of meat cooked in their own juice, or of smaller pieces packed on skewers and grilled or roasted, or minced and ground in a paste and formed into oval cutlets and fried. Sometimes they are pressed on to skewers and grilled.

Shikampooree Kabab

In a little ghee or other fat, fry for 3 or 4 minutes: 1 onion, 2 cloves of garlic, a 12 mm ($\frac{1}{2}$ inch) piece of fresh or pickled ginger and 2 fresh or pickled chillies (all chopped very finely).

Then add:

A handful of green coriander leaves well washed and dried or 1 teaspoonful of ground corianders.
1 teaspoonful of ground turmeric.
$\frac{1}{2}$ teaspoonful of ground cummin seed.
$\frac{1}{2}$ teaspoonful of ground almonds.
$\frac{1}{2}$ teaspoonful of ground cheroonjee.
$\frac{1}{2}$ teaspoonful of ground allspice.
A large pinch of ground cinnamon.
A large pinch of ground cardamoms.
A small pinch of ground cloves.
1 tablespoonful of Chenna flour (Basun).

Mix thoroughly and continue the slow cooking for about 5 minutes longer. Then add 450 g (1 lb) of finely minced lean meat and 1 tablespoonful of thick cocoanut milk. Cook for 10 minutes longer. Salt to taste. Turn out the contents of pan and either grind or pound this mixture into a fine paste.

Blend together dry curds (Dhye) and fresh mint with a pinch of salt. Then take sufficient meat paste to form a ball the size of a billard ball, and depress this ball gradually in the palm of your hand until you produce a shallow depression, in which you place ½ teaspoonful of the curds or Dhye mixture. Then gradually work the meat upwards until the curd is covered completely and you have a round flat cutlet. These cutlets are fried a golden brown.

Moglai Hoosaini Kabab (*Spicy*)

Add to 450 g (1 lb) of very finely minced lean mutton, 4 green chillies, 2 cloves of garlic, 1 large onion, and a 12 mm (½ inch) piece of fresh or pickled ginger (all minced very finely).

Fry the following ingredients lightly for 2 or 3 minutes in a dessertspoonful of ghee or other fat:

1 dessertspoonful of desiccated cocoanut.
1 teaspoonful of ground almonds.
1 teaspoonful of Chenna flour (Basun).
1 teaspoonful of ground corianders.
1 teaspoonful of ground turmeric.
A small pinch of ground cinnamon.
A small pinch of ground cloves.
A small pinch of ground cardamoms.
A small pinch of ground allspice.

Mix, add the meat mixture, stir thoroughly and continue the slow cooking for 5 to 10 minutes. Salt to taste. Turn the contents out and either grind or pound this meat mixture into a fine paste, adding a squeeze of lemon juice. The paste is formed into oval-shaped cutlets and fried a golden brown, or pressed on to metal skewers and grilled, basting well.

Sami Kabab (*Spicy*)

450 g (1 lb) of finely minced lean mutton,
1 dessertspoonful of ground corianders.
1 teaspoonful of ground turmeric.
½ teaspoonful of ground ginger.
½ teaspoonful of ground chillies.
½ teaspoonful of ground Kus Kus.
1 teaspoonful of fine desiccated cocoanut.
1 pinch of ground cloves.
1 pinch of ground cinnamon.

1 pinch of ground cardamoms.

1 dessertspoonful of ground Chenna flour (Bengal Gram) *or* ordinary flour.

Salt to taste.

Make a mixture of the above ingredients.

In a stewpan warm 56 g (2 ozs) of ghee or other fat and fry lightly in it 2 small onions and 2 cloves of garlic, both finely minced.

Add to this the above mixture, stir well and cook slowly for 10 or 15 minutes. Turn out, let it cool, and then either grind or pound it into a paste with a squeeze of lemon juice. Form into oval cutlets and fry in the usual way, or press on to metal skewers and grill, basting well.

Moglai Sami Kabab (*Plain*)

56 g (2 ozs) of ghee or other fat.

1 tablespoonful of Korma mixture.

½ teaspoonful of ground turmeric.

3 or 4 finely chopped fresh or pickled chillies.

½ teaspoonful of finely chopped fresh or pickled green ginger.

2 cloves of garlic, finely minced.

1 onion, finely minced.

Fry lightly in the ghee or other fat all the above ingredients for 3 or 4 minutes, then add to it 450 g (1 lb) of finely minced fresh, lean mutton or beef and cook for 10 minutes on a slow fire with the pan uncovered. Add a tablespoonful of Chenna (Bengal gram flour) or other flour. Salt and lemon juice to taste.

Turn the mixture out to cool, then grind or pound it into a fine paste, shape into oval cutlets and fry in the usual way, or press on to metal skewers and grill, basting well.

Dry Hoosaini Kababas

450 g (1 lb) of very finely minced beef or mutton.

1 medium sized onion ⎫
2 or 3 cloves of garlic ⎭ minced very finely.

½ teaspoonful of ground chillies.

½ teaspoonful of ground ginger.

1 teaspoonful of ground turmeric.

1 saltspoonful of ground cinnamon.

1 saltspoonful of ground cardamoms.
A small pinch of ground cloves.
Pepper and salt to taste.

Blend all the above ingredients together with an egg. Shape them into oval cutlets and fry in boiling ghee or other fat.

Devilled Kabab Curry – Shythani Kabab Ka Salun

450 g (1 lb) of lean mutton cut up into 12 mm (½ inch) squares and packed on to wooden skewers alternately with button onions or small shallots, cut in halves, and sliced green ginger, with occasionally here and there a thin slice of garlic.

Sprinkle over with cayenne pepper, and gently fry in ghee or other fat for about 10 minutes, then drain

In a *sauté* pan fry lightly in the fat in which the Kababs have been fried:

2 tablespoonfuls of chopped onion.
½ small teaspoonful of chopped garlic.
3 or 4 fresh or pickled chillies, cut lengthwise.

Then add a heaped tablespoonful of curry powder and a dessertspoonful of tomato paste or purée. Mix well and continue the cooking for 3 or 4 minutes longer

Then with a very little water convert it into a thickish gravy. Now add the skewers of meat. Cover the pan, shake it occasionally and cook slowly until the meat is quite done. Salt and lemon juice to taste.

A delicious but very hot curry.

Kooftah Kabab

450 g (1 lb) of fresh mutton or beef freed from skin and fat
    and minced very finely.
1 tablespoonful of Kooftah mixture.
1 tablespoonful of finely chopped onion.
½ teaspoonful of very finely chopped garlic.
1 egg.
1 dessertspoonful of Dhye (sour curds).
Butter or ghee.
1 tablespoonful of flour.
Salt.

Partially cook in sufficient butter or ghee the onions and garlic, then add the Kooftah mixture. Mix well and cook for 4 or 5 minutes longer on a slow fire. Remove from the fire and let the mixture cool down, then add to it the meat, Dhye, egg, flour and salt to taste. Mix thoroughly, and taking up a heaped tablespoonful of the mixture, either shape it into oval cutlets and fry in ghee or other fat, or preferably cover small skewers with the mixture and either grill or roast before a charcoal fire, basting well.

Marinade for Kababs

Pound in a mortar:

2 or 3 tablespoonfuls of chopped onions.
4 cloves of garlic, and add gradually to it:
1 dessertspoonful of ground corianders.
1 teaspoonful of ground turmeric.
1 teaspoonful of ground Kus Kus.
½ teaspoonful of ground chillies.
½ teaspoonful of ground ginger.

Now stir into it a tablespoonful or more of mustard, gingili or olive oil and 285 ml (½ pint) of thick Tyre (sour curds). Lemon juice and salt to taste. Blend all well together.

Moglai Kabab

450 g (1 lb) of lean mutton cut up in large pieces is marinaded for an hour or two in the Marinade for Kababs. (See above).

The whole is then turned, to a saucepan and, without any additional moisture, cooked slowly until the meat is quite tender. Add salt to taste.

Stick Kabab (Seekh Kabab)

450 g (1 lb) of lean mutton, cut up in 25 mm (1 inch) squares and marinaded in the Kabab marinade (see above) for an hour or two. Then pack on wooden or metal skewers, 100 to 125 mm (4 to 5 inches) long, alternate pieces of the meat from the marinade, tiny button onions, and thin slices of green or pickled ginger until the skewer is tightly packed, leaving the ends free for roasting before the fire or grilling over it. Baste well.

Plain Stick Kababs (Seekh Kababs)

450 g (1 lb) of lean mutton or beef, freed from fat and skin. Cut the meat up into even pieces about 25 mm (1 inch) square and 12 mm ($\frac{1}{2}$ inch) thick and marinade it for 2 or more hours in the marinade for Kababs. (See page 45).

Take 100 mm (4 inch) skewers and pack on six pieces of meat. Grill over a charcoal fire or on an ordinary grill, basting them frequently with ghee or oiled butter until cooked.

These Kababs are eaten dry with Chuppaties, but they can also be served with plain rice or Kitcheree. A gravy in that case is made by frying in ghee or butter the ingredients which formed the marinade.

Goanese Stick Kabab

450 g (1 lb) of lean mutton and 450 g (1 lb) of pork cut up in 25 mm (1 inch) squares and packed alternately on 100 to 125 mm (4 to 5 inch) wooden skewers with thin slices of green or pickled ginger between them.

In 56 g (2 ozs) of ghee or other fat lightly fry for 2 or 3 minutes:

1 large onion
3 or 4 cloves of garlic   }   sliced finely.
6 fresh or pickled chillies cut lengthwise.

Add to this a heaped tablespoonful of Vindaloo mixture. Mix and blend with it a dessertspoonful of tomato paste or purée, gradually thinning it down with a little tarmarind water to a thick gravy in which the packed skewers of meat are cooked until tender. Salt to taste.

Dry Kababs of Mutton and Pork

(Indo-Portuguese)

225 g ($\frac{1}{2}$ lb) of pork and 225 g ($\frac{1}{2}$ lb) of mutton are cut up into 25 mm (1 inch) cubes and packed on metal skewers alternately with thin slices of green ginger and small button onions. Sprinkle over with black pepper and salt. Grill over or before a charcoal fire and baste well whilst grilling. Squeeze lemon juice to taste over the Kababs before serving.

Hurran Ka Gosht Kabab

Steaks of well-hung venison.
    Make a paste with either vinegar or lemon juice of:
        1 dessertspoonful of ground turmeric.
        $\frac{1}{2}$ teaspoonful of ground chillies.
        Salt to taste.
    Rub this thoroughly into the steaks and either grill or fry.

VII

Chicken, Duck and Game Curries

Ceylon Chicken Curry

1 chicken, jointed.

1 onion and
2 cloves of garlic } finely minced.

3 or 4 fresh green or red or pickled chillies, cut lengthwise.

1 teaspoonful of ground turmeric.

1 dessertspoonful of ground corianders or a handful of picked green coriander leaves.

1 tablespoonful of ghee.

570 ml (1 pint) thick cocoanut milk.

570 ml (1 pint) of thin cocoanut milk.

Warm the ghee and add all the above ingredients except the chicken and the cocoanut milk.

Fry for 2 or 3 minutes. Then add the chicken and a pint of thin cocoanut milk. Simmer slowly until the chicken is tender, then add the thick cocoanut milk. Salt to taste and a squeeze of lemon juice. Simmer for another 5 minutes, taking care to keep the pan uncovered during the whole process.

Madras Chicken Curry

Joint the chicken (a small one).

Fry lightly in 56 g (2 ozs) of ghee or other fat, 2 heaped table-spoonfuls of chopped onions, and 2 cloves of garlic chopped up. Cook until the onions begin to change colour, then add a heaped tablespoonful of curry powder, stir well, and fry this mixture for 3 or 4 minutes.

Now add the jointed chicken, stir thoroughly and, covering the pan, cook slowly for as long as possible without adding any moisture. Should the curry be getting dry, then add gradually a little water or stock to form a thickish gravy.

Simmer slowly until the meat is tender, and a richness appears on the surface of the curry. A great improvement is to add a tablespoonful of tomato paste (or 225 g ($\frac{1}{2}$ lb) of fresh tomatoes chopped up) whilst the meat is cooking.

Salt and lemon juice to taste.

Chicken Curry

Ingredients for the curry:

1 tablespoonful of ground corianders. ⎫
1 teaspoonful of ground mustard seed. ⎪
1 teaspoonful of ground cummin seed. ⎬ mixed
1 teaspoonful of ground turmeric. ⎪ together
½ teaspoonful of ground ginger. ⎪
½ teaspoonful of ground chillies. ⎭

Cook, but do not brown, 1 onion and 2 cloves of garlic, finely chopped together, in 1 tablespoonful of ghee or other fat. Add to it the curry mixture and fry in it for 5 minutes one jointed chicken. To form the gravy, add thin cocoanut milk just sufficient to cover the chicken. Simmer gently with the pan uncovered until the gravy begins to thicken and the chicken is tender. Then add a tablespoonful of thick cocoanut milk. Salt to taste and a squeeze of lemon juice.

Chicken Curry

(Another way)

1 chicken, jointed.
1 onion ⎫
1 clove of garlic ⎬ finely sliced.
56 g (2 ozs) of ghee or other fat.
2 cardamoms.
2 cloves.
A 50 mm (2 inch) stick of cinnamon.
1 tablespoonful of ground corianders.
1 teaspoonful of ground turmeric.
½ teaspoonful of ground ginger.
½ teaspoonful of ground cummin seed.
¼ teaspoonful or rather less of ground chillies.
A saltspoonful of ground fenugreek.

Fry in the ghee or other fat the onions, garlic, cloves, cardamoms, and cinnamon, but do not let the onions brown. When sufficiently cooked add all the other ingredients. Mix well and cook on a slow fire for 4 or 5 minutes. Then add the jointed chicken and let it fry in this curry mixture for a few minutes, but take care that it does not catch.

Add sufficient water to form a thickish gravy, cover the pan and simmer until the chicken is cooked. A squeeze of lemon juice or a little tamarind pulp and salt to taste is now added.

Chicken Curry

(Another way)

1 chicken, jointed.
1 onion ⎫
2 cloves of garlic ⎭ finely sliced.
56 g (2 ozs) of ghee or other fat.
3 dessertspoonfuls of ground corianders.
1 heaped teaspoonful of ground turmeric.
½ teaspoonful of ground ginger.
¼ teaspoonful of ground chillies.
285 ml (½ pint) of thin cocoanut milk.

Fry lightly in the fat for 3 or 4 minutes the onions and garlic, then add the ground ingredients and cook for 2 or 3 minutes longer. Add the jointed chicken and thin cocoanut milk. Mix well and with the pan uncovered let the contents simmer until the chicken is cooked.

If necessary, add a little water, and just before serving add salt to taste and 2 tablespoonfuls of thick cocoanut milk.

Chicken Curry

(Another way)

1 chicken, jointed and marinaded for an hour or two in the following mixture:

285 ml (½ pint) of sour curds (Dhye).
2 heaped dessertspoonfuls of ground corianders.
1 heaped teaspoonful of ground turmeric.
½ teaspoonful of ground cummin seed.
½ teaspoonful of ground chillies.
1 saltspoonful of ground fenugreek.
2 tablespoonfuls of finely minced onion.
1 clove of garlic, finely minced.

Fry in 56 g (2 ozs) of ghee or other fat for 2 or 3 minutes, 1 onion, and 1 clove of garlic, sliced finely, 3 cloves, 3 cardamoms, and a 50 mm (2 inch) stick of cinnamon.

Add to this the chicken and the whole of the marinade. Mix, cover the pan closely, and let the contents simmer until the chicken is cooked. Care must be taken that sufficient liquor is formed in the pan to prevent it from burning and to make a thick rich gravy.

This curry is finished by adding salt to taste, a squeeze of lemon juice and a tablespoonful of either freshly scraped cocoanut or finely desiccated cocoanut.

Chicken Curry

(Another way)

1 chicken cut up.
56 g (2 ozs) of ghee.
2 tablespoons of chopped onion.
1 clove of garlic, finely sliced.

Blend into a paste with cocoanut milk:

1 tablespoonful of ground corianders.
1 teaspoonful of ground turmeric.
½ teaspoonful of ground cummin seed.
½ teaspoonful of ground black pepper.
½ teaspoonful of ground chillies.
1 dessertspoonful of finely desiccated cocoanut.
½ teaspoonful of ground mustard seed.
¼ teaspoonful of ground fenugreek.

Fry lightly in the ghee for 3 or 4 minutes the onion and garlic. Add the paste as above. Mix, continue the cooking for a further 3 or 4 minutes. Now add the jointed chicken. Cover the pan closely and simmer until the meat is tender. Watch the pan in case the gravy dries up, and add water or stock if necessary. Salt and lemon juice to taste.

Hyderabad Chicken Curry with Sliced Cocoanut

1 chicken, jointed.
½ a fresh cocoanut sliced with the outer skin removed.
1 onion ⎫
2 cloves of garlic ⎬ minced finely.
2 cardamoms.
2 cloves.

A 25 mm (2 inch) stick of cinnamon.

1 heaped tablespoonful of curry powder.

1 dessertspoonful of curry paste.

56 g (2 ozs) of ghee or other fat.

1 heaped tablespoonful of tomato paste or 225 g ($\frac{1}{2}$ lb) of fresh tomatoes peeled and well chopped.

Fry lightly for 2 or 3 minutes in the ghee or other fat, the onions, garlic and spices. Then add the curry powder and curry paste. Mix thoroughly and continue the frying for another 3 or 4 minutes.

Add the tomato and jointed chicken, the sliced cocoanut and about 285 ml ($\frac{1}{2}$ pint) of water to form a thickish gravy. Mix thoroughly, cover the pan closely, and let the contents simmer until the chicken is tender. Add salt and a squeeze of lemon juice to taste.

Chicken Curry with Greens

1 chicken, jointed.

1 onion

1 clove of garlic } chopped finely.

56 g (2 ozs) of ghee.

2 heaped dessertspoonfuls of curry paste.

$\frac{1}{2}$ teaspoonful of ground fenugreek.

2 cardamoms.

2 cloves.

A 50 mm (2 inch) stick of cinnamon.

1 dessertspoonful of ground almonds, or a teaspoonful of ground poppy seeds (Kus Kus)

Thick cocoanut milk.

2 handfuls of picked Methe Bhagi or shredded lettuce.

Fry lightly in the ghee for 3 or 4 minutes, the onions, garlic and spices. Then add the curry paste, fenugreek and either ground almonds or ground Kus Kus. Mix thoroughly. Continue the frying for 3 or 4 minutes longer. Add the jointed chicken, mix again. Cover the pan, simmer gently for 10 or 15 minutes. Watch carefully that the contents do not burn. If too dry add a little water. Now add the Methe Bhagi or lettuce, previously well washed and drained, and, mixing lightly, simmer until the chicken is cooked. Salt and lemon juice to taste.

N.B. – Methe Bhagi can be easily grown under glass or in the

open in the summer from Methee (or fenugreek) seeds. If unobtainable, shredded lettuce, turnip tops, broccoli, etc., can be
used in place of it.

Chicken and Dhall Curry

1 chicken, jointed.
113 g ($\frac{1}{4}$ lb) of Moosa Dhall or Egyptian lentils.
2 dry red chillies.
1 onion
2 cloves of garlic } finely sliced.
1 heaped tablespoonful of curry powder.
1 dessertspoonful of condensed tomato paste or 225 g ($\frac{1}{2}$ lb)
    of fresh tomatoes peeled and chopped up.
56 g (2 ozs) of ghee or other fat.
1 tablespoonful of desiccated cocoanut.

Wash the Dhall or lentils thoroughly and set to boil with the dry
chillies in about 285 ml ($\frac{1}{2}$ pint) or a little more of cold water until
the lentils are more than half cooked.

Fry lightly, in the fat, the onions and garlic for 2 or 3 minutes.
Then add the curry powder. Mix well, and cook on a slow fire
for a further 3 or 4 minutes. Now add the tomato and then the
jointed chicken. Mix, cover the pan, and cook on a slow fire for
10 or 15 minutes, taking care to prevent the contents from
burning.

Add the boiled lentils – which must not be strained – and
continue with the simmering with the pan covered until cooked.
Add the cocoanut, a dessertspoonful of tamarind pulp or other
acid and salt to taste.

Chicken Curry with Chenna Dhall

Half teacupful of Chenna Dhall soaked overnight, drained and
put into sufficient fresh cold water and boiled until cooked, but
not pulped.

Fry lightly for 2 or 3 minutes in 56 g (2 ozs) of ghee or other fat:
    2 tablespoonfuls of chopped onion.
    1 clove of garlic, sliced finely.
    4 cardamoms.
    4 cloves.
    A 50 mm (2 inch) stick of cinnamon.

Add 2 heaped dessertspoonfuls of curry paste and 1 dessert-spoonful of ground almonds. Mix thoroughly and cook for a further 4 or 5 minutes.

Add the jointed chicken and let it fry in this mixture for another 15 minutes. Then add ½ teacupful of thick cocoanut milk and let it simmer with the pan uncovered until the chicken is tender. Add the Chenna Dhall, lemon juice and salt to taste. Simmer for another 5 minutes before serving.

N.B. – If this curry is too rich, use curry powder instead of curry paste, or equal parts of each.

Dry Chicken Curry

1 chicken, jointed.
2 onions ⎫
2 cloves of garlic ⎬ finely sliced.
2 dessertspoonfuls of curry paste.
1 dessertspoonful of tomato paste or purée.
56 g (2 ozs) of ghee or other fat.

Fry lightly in the ghee for 2 or 3 minutes the onions and garlic. Add the curry and tomato paste, and continue the frying for another 2 or 3 minutes. Then add the chicken. Mix well, cover the pan closely, and simmer until the chicken is cooked.

The pan must be continually watched, as the contents are likely to catch. If this appears likely, add just sufficient water to prevent it.

Add salt and lemon juice to taste, and a tablespoonful of finely desiccated cocoanut which will absorb any excessive gravy.

Dry Curry of Cold Chicken

Fry in ghee or other fat for 2 or 3 minutes:
2 tablespoonfuls of onion.
2 cloves of garlic, minced finely.
1 heaped teaspoonful of ground turmeric.
½ teaspoonful of ground cummin seed.
½ teaspoonful of ground chillies.
½ teaspoonful of ground ginger.

Add 2 or 3 fresh tomatoes, peeled and chopped finely. Mix well and simmer for 10 minutes on a slow fire. Then add lemon juice and salt to taste and lastly the cold chicken, and let it warm through thoroughly.

Dry Curry of Cold Chicken, etc.

Use the legs of cold poultry of any sort for this purpose.

In a rather shallow *sauté* pan fry lightly in 56 g (2 ozs) of ghee for 2 or 3 minutes:

> 2 tablespoonfuls of chopped onion.
> ½ teaspoonful of chopped garlic.
> 2 or 3 fresh or pickled chillies, cut lengthwise.
> 6 thin slices of fresh, green or pickled ginger.

Now add to this a heaped tablespoonful of curry powder and a heaped dessertspoonful of finely desiccated cocoanut.

Mix and continue the frying for 2 or 3 minutes longer. Then add the jointed chicken and, mixing lightly, warm through thoroughly. Lemon juice and salt to taste.

Cold Poultry or Game Curry

Usually the legs of cold chicken, duck, turkey, geese or game are used up in this fashion. The thick sauce or gravy is made of the following ingredients, the cold material added and gently warmed through.

To Make the Sauce

Fry lightly in 56 g (2 ozs) of ghee or other fat for 2 or 3 minutes: 2 tablespoonfuls of chopped onion and ½ teaspoonful of chopped garlic. Add a tablespoonful of curry powder, or, if preferred rich, 2 dessertspoonfuls of curry paste. Blend thoroughly with the onion and continue the cooking for another 3 or 4 minutes. Add a heaped dessertspoonful of tomato paste or purée, and mix and then thin down with a little water or stock to a thickish gravy. Salt and lemon juice to taste. Simmer for 10 minutes before adding the cold material.

Rabbit Curry (Kurghosh Ka Salun)

> 1 rabbit jointed up, well washed and soaked in salt and water for 10 minutes or so.
> 1 large onion ⎫
> 2 cloves of garlic ⎭ minced finely.
> 1 heaped tablespoonful of curry powder.
> 1 dessertspoonful of tomato paste or purée.
> Salt and lemon juice to taste.

Fry lightly in 84 g (3 ozs) of ghee or other fat for 3 or 4 minutes the onions and garlic, then add the curry paste and continue the cooking for another few minutes, gradually adding to it the tomato paste mixed with a little water.

Add the rabbit, mix well and simmer gently, but do not let it dry, and when necessary add stock or water to form a thick gravy. Cover the pan and continue the simmering until the rabbit is quite tender. Salt and lemon juice to taste.

Milk instead of water may be used to form the gravy.

Wild rabbit and hare are curried in exactly the same way, but a better result is obtained by using curry paste instead of curry powder.

Duck Curry (*Vathoo Curry*)

In a tablespoonful or more of ghee or other fat, fry lightly 1 onion and 1 clove of garlic, both finely sliced. Then add:

2 tablespoonfuls of ground corianders.
2 teaspoonfuls of ground turmeric.
½ teaspoonful of ground cummin seed.
½ teaspoonful of ground fenugreek.
½ teaspoonful of ground ginger.
½ teaspoonful of ground chillies.

Mix well and now fry in this mixture for 4 or 5 minutes a duck cut up into convenient pieces. Cover the pan and continue cooking on a slow fire for a few more minutes. Then add 570 ml (1 pint) of water and let the curry simmer until the duck is tender. Add salt and lemon juice to taste and a tablespoonful of thick cocoanut milk.

Deccan Duck Curry (*Budhuk Ka Salun*)

1 fat duck cut up into convenient pieces.
1 large onion ⎫
1 or 2 cloves of garlic ⎬ finely sliced.
2 or more ordinary cloves.
A 50 mm (2 inch) stick of cinnamon.
2 or 3 cardamoms.
3 dessertspoonfuls of curry powder or equal parts of curry powder and curry paste.

Fry lightly in 56 g (2 ozs) of ghee or other fat, the onions, garlic, cloves, cinnamon and cardamoms. Now add the curry powder or the powder and paste. Stir thoroughly and continue the frying for 3 or 4 minutes. Then add the duck and sufficient water to form a thickish gravy.

Mix well, cover the pan closely and simmer until the duck is tender. Two tablespoonfuls of thick cocoanut milk, salt and lemon juice to taste are added just before serving.

Madras Duck Curry (Vathoo Curry)

In 56 g (2 ozs) of ghee or other fat lightly fry 1 onion and 1 clove of garlic, both finely sliced, and 2 or 3 fresh or pickled chillies, cut lengthwise in halves. Then add to it 3 dessertspoonfuls of curry powder or curry paste and ½ a teaspoonful of bruised cummin seed. Mix thoroughly and continue the cooking for 3 or 4 minutes.

Now add a fat duck, jointed or cut up into convenient pieces. Stir the whole thoroughly and add sufficient water to form a thickish gravy. Cover the pan closely and simmer until the duck is cooked. Add salt and lemon juice to taste and 1 tablespoonful or so of thick cocoanut milk just before serving.

Duck and Green Pea Curry (Budhuk Aur Mutter)

1 duck, jointed up into convenient pieces.
1 breakfast cupful of partially cooked green peas.
225 g (½ lb) of tomatoes.
1 large onion ⎫
1 clove of garlic ⎬ finely minced.
3 dessertspoonfuls of curry powder.
56 g (2 ozs) of ghee or other fat.

Fry the onions and garlic in the fat for 2 or 3 minutes, but do not let them brown. Add the curry powder, mix well and continue the cooking on a slow fire for 3 or 4 minutes longer. Then add the fresh tomatoes, peeled and chopped up, or a tablespoonful of tomato purée and about 570 ml (1 pint) water. Mix thoroughly and, adding the jointed duck, cover the pan and continue the cooking until the meat is tender. Add the peas and finish the dish when the peas are cooked by adding salt and lemon juice to taste.

Wild Duck Curry (*Jungli Budhuk Ka Salun*)

1 duck, divided into 4 portions.

56 g (2 ozs) of ghee.

2 tablespoonfuls of chopped onions.

1 clove of garlic, finely minced.

2 green or pickled chillies, slit lengthwise.

1 tablespoonful of curry paste.

2 tablespoonfuls of thick cocoanut milk.

1 heaped dessertspoonful of tomato paste.

Fry lightly for a minute or two in the ghee, the onions, garlic and green chillies. Then add the curry and tomato paste. Mix well and continue the cooking for 2 or 3 minutes longer.

Add the duck and a teacupful or more of water. Mix, cover the pan, and simmer gently until the bird is cooked.

Add the cocoanut milk and, with the pan uncovered, simmer for another few minutes. Salt and lemon juice to taste.

VIII

Mutton, Lamb, Beef and Pork Curries

Stick Curry (Seekh Kabab Ka Salun)

Prepared as for grilling, but cooked in curry form.

In a *sauté* pan fry lightly in 56 g (2 ozs) of ghee or other fat for 3 or 4 minutes:

2 tablespoonfuls of chopped onion.
1 clove of garlic (minced finely).
2 ordinary cloves.
2 whole cardamoms.
A 50 mm (2 inch) stick of cinnamon.

Add to it a dessertspoonful of curry powder. Continue the frying for 2 or 3 minutes longer, then add the whole of the marinade (see p. 45). Mix well and place in this the skewers of meat. Cover the pan and simmer the contents (shaking the pan occasionally) until the meat is cooked. Salt to taste.

If the gravy is too thick, add a little stock or water.

Madras Stick Curry

Pack tightly on 100 to 125 mm (4 to 5 inch) skewers 450g (1 lb) of lean mutton or beef cut up into 25-mm (1-inch) cubes, alternately with thin slices of green ginger and tiny button onions.

Fry lightly in 56 g (2 ozs) of ghee or other fat for 2 or 3 minutes:

2 tablespoonfuls of chopped onion.
1 or 2 cloves of garlic sliced finely.
2 or 3 fresh or pickled chillies, cut lengthwise.

Add to this a tablespoonful of curry powder. Mix well and continue the cooking for another minute or two, then stir in a dessertspoonful of tomato paste or purée and gradually thin it down with stock or water to a thickish gravy.

Pack the skewers of meat in this gravy. Cover the pan and simmer gently until the meat is tender. Salt and lemon juice to taste.

Madras Stick Curry

(Another way)

450 g (1 lb) of beef or mutton. Pack on wooden skewers small pieces of meat with tiny onions and slices of fresh green or pickled ginger alternately.

1 tablespoonful of ghee or other fat.
1 small onion ⎫
1 clove of garlic ⎭ chopped finely.
1 dessertspoonful of ground corianders.
1 teaspoonful of ground turmeric.
½ teaspoonful of ground fresh green ginger.
Rather less than ½ teaspoonful of ground chillies.
285 ml (½ pint) of Tyre (sour curds).

Fry the above ingredients, excepting the Tyre, in the ghee or other fat for 5 minutes. Then add the skewers of meat and let them fry in the mixture, but take care that they do not burn. Add the Tyre and sufficient water to cover the meat and form the gravy. Closely cover the pan and simmer on a slow fire until the meat is tender. Salt to taste before serving.

Pork Curry (Punny Curry)

450 g (1 lb) of pork, cut up into convenient pieces.
1 onion ⎫
2 cloves of garlic ⎭ finely minced.
4 fresh or pickled chillies, cut lengthwise.
8 thin slices of green ginger.
3 or 4 cloves.
3 or 4 cardamoms.
A 50 mm (2 inch) stick of cinnamon.

Fry lightly all the above ingredients, except the pork, in 56 g (2 ozs) of ghee or other fat, and then add the following:

1 dessertspoonful of ground corianders ⎫ made into
1 teaspoonful of ground turmeric ⎪ a paste with
½ teaspoonful of ground cummin seed ⎬ a little
½ teaspoonful of ground chillies ⎭ vinegar.

Mix well and fry for another 2 or 3 minutes on a slow fire.
Add the pork and continue the frying without increasing the

heat, and then gradually add sufficient thin tamarind water to form a fair amount of gravy. Cover the pan and simmer until the meat is cooked. Salt to taste.

Mutton or Beef Curry with Sour Curds

This is either a beef or mutton curry cooked in sour curds, and consequently is a rich curry.

450 g (1 lb) of meat cup up into convenient sizes is marinaded for 2 or 3 hours in the following marinade:

1 onion	
2 cloves of garlic	all
2 or 3 fresh green or red or pickled chillies	finely
6 thin slices of green ginger	chopped
A handful of green coriander leaves	and
1 teaspoonful of ground turmeric	pounded.
½ teaspoonful of ground cinnamon	

All blended together in a pint of sour curds.

Fry, but do not brown, another sliced onion in a tablespoonful of ghee or other fat, then add the meat and marinade. Mix, cover the pan closely and let the contents simmer until the meat is tender. Add salt to taste.

Drumstick Curry (Mooroongakai Curry)

450 g (1 lb) of mutton cut up in convenient pieces; 6 drumsticks cup up in 75 mm (3 inch) lengths and tied together in bundles of 6 pieces.

Fry lightly for 2 or 3 minutes in 56 g (2 ozs) of ghee or other fat:

1 onion	finely chopped.
2 cloves of garlic	

Then add:

1 heaped dessertspoonful of curry powder.
½ teaspoonful of ground cummin seed.
½ teaspoonful of ground turmeric.

and continue the cooking for another 3 or 4 minutes. Add the meat, stir thoroughly, cover the pan and cook slowly for 10 minutes or so.

Now add gradually a little water or thin cocoanut milk to form the gravy and, with the pan uncovered, bring to the boil and simmer until the meat is more than half cooked. Add the drumsticks and continue the cooking until both the meat and drumsticks are thoroughly cooked. Salt and lemon juice to taste and a tablespoonful of thick cocoanut milk.

Madras Mutton Curry (*Ahtoo Curry*)

450 g (1 lb) of lean uncooked mutton, cut up in convenient pieces.

Fry lightly in 56 g (2 ozs) of ghee or other fat for 2 or 3 minutes: 2 heaped tablespoonfuls of chopped onions and 1 clove of garlic, very finely chopped. Cook until the onions begin to change colour, then add a heaped tablespoonful of curry powder, stir well and fry this mixture for 3 or 4 minutes. Then add the uncooked meat and a tablespoonful or more of tomato paste. Stir again thoroughly, cover the pan, and cook slowly as long as possible without adding any moisture.

Should the curry be getting dry, then add a little water or stock to form a thickish gravy. Add salt and lemon juice to taste and simmer slowly until the meat is tender and a richness appears on the surface of the curry.

Deccan Beef or Mutton Curry (*Ghosht Ka Salun*)

450 g (1 lb) of mutton or beef cup up as desired and mixed with the following ingredients:

1 large onion, minced finely.
1 tablespoonful of ground corianders.
1 heaped teaspoonful of ground turmeric.
½ teaspoonful of ground cummin seed.
½ teaspoonful of ground pepper.
6 thin slices of green ginger.
2 fresh green or pickled chillies, chopped finely.
A pinch of ground chillies.
1 dessertspoonful of freshly desiccated cocoanut.

Fry lightly in 56 g (2 ozs) of ghee or other fat for 3 or 4 minutes, 1 onion and a clove of garlic, finely minced, then add the meat mixed in the curry ingredients as above.

Cook on a slow fire for 4 or 5 minutes, and then add 285 ml (½ pint) of water. Simmer gently, with the pan covered, until the meat is tender. Ten minutes before serving, add salt to taste and ½ a teacupful of thick cocoanut milk.

Beef Curry (Madoo Curry)

450 g (1 lb) of beef, cut up into convenient pieces.
1 tablespoonful of ground corianders.
1 teaspoonful of ground turmeric.
½ teaspoonful of ground cummin seed.
¼ teaspoonful of ground chillies.
A generous pinch of ground fenugreek.
A generous pinch of ground black pepper.
A generous pinch of ground mustard seed.

(All these ingredients made into a stiff paste with a little weak vinegar or weak tamarind water.)

In 28 g (1 oz) of ghee or other fat, fry lightly for 3 or 4 minutes, an onion and a clove of garlic, finely sliced. Add the other ingredients except the beef and continue the frying for 2 or 3 minutes longer. Now add the meat, stir well and cook slowly until a thickish gravy appears. Add to it less than 285 ml (½ pint) of water, cover the pan and let the curry simmer until the meat is thoroughly cooked.

Add ½ teacupful of thin cocoanut milk and salt to taste and, with the pan uncovered, continue the simmering for another few minutes.

Madras Beef Curry (Madoo Curry)

450 g (1 lb) of beef cut up into convenient pieces.
1 onion
1 clove of garlic ⎱ minced finely.
1 dry chillie (seeds removed) ⎰
28 g (1 oz) of ghee or other fat.
1 tablespoonful of curry powder.
1 dessertspoonful of tomato paste or purée, or 2 or 3 fresh tomatoes peeled and chopped finely.

Fry the chopped ingredients in the ghee or other fat for 3 or 4 minutes. Then add the curry powder. Stir and continue the frying for another 3 or 4 minutes.

Add the meat, mix well and cook for a few minutes longer. Now add the tomato paste or tomato and 285 ml (½ pint) of water or stock. Cover the pan, bring to the boil and simmer gently until the meat is cooked. The gravy should be thick. Salt and lemon juice to taste.

This curry can be made richer by using equal parts of curry paste and curry powder, or it can be made entirely of curry paste. In either of these cases no additional acid will be needed.

Calcutta Beef Curry (Ghosht Ka Salun)

450 g (1 lb) of lean beef, cut into convenient pieces and simmered in 570 ml (1 pint) of water until tender.

Make into a paste with a little thin cocoanut milk the following ingredients:

1 tablespoonful of ground corianders.
½ teaspoonful of ground turmeric.
½ teaspoonful of ground cummin seed.
½ teaspoonful of ground chillies.
A pinch of black pepper.
A pinch of ground ginger.

In 28 g (1 oz) of ghee or other fat, fry lightly an onion and a clove of garlic, sliced finely. Add the paste and continue the frying for 2 or 3 minutes longer. Then add the meat, together with a little of the broth. Bring gradually to the boil and add 285 ml (½ pint) of thick cocoanut milk. Salt and lemon juice to taste.

Beef and Dhall Curry (Dhall Cha)

450 g (1 lb) of lean beef cut up into convenient pieces.

113 g (¼ lb) of Dhall or Egyptian lentils
2 dry red chillies (seeds removed) } par-boiled in 285 ml (1 pint) of water and drained.

1 onion
1 clove of garlic } chopped finely.
2 cardamoms.
2 cloves.
1 25 mm (1 inch) stick of cinnamon.
1 tablespoonful of curry powder.
1 dessertspoonful of tomato paste.
28 g (1 oz) of ghee or other fat.

Fry lightly in the ghee or other fat for 3 or 4 minutes, the onions, garlic and spices, then add the curry powder and continue the cooking on a slow fire for a few minutes longer. Add the tomato paste, mix well, add the meat and cook for 3 or 4 minutes longer.

Now add the water in which the Dhall has been boiled. Bring to the boil, cover the pan and simmer gently until the meat is nearly cooked. Add the par-boiled Dhall. Salt to taste and a teaspoonful of thick tarmarind pulp or vinegar. With the pan covered, continue the cooking until the meat is tender and the Dhall is completely cooked.

Madras Dhall and Meat Curry (Dhall Cha)

450 g (1 lb) of meat cut up into convenient sizes.
113 g (¼ lb) of Mussoor Dhall or Egyptian lentils.
1 tablespoonful of ground corianders.
½ teaspoonful of ground cummin seed.
½ teaspoonful of ground red chillies.
½ teaspoonful of ground ginger.
1 teaspoonful of ground turmeric.
1 tablespoonful of ghee or other fat.
1 large onion
2 cloves of garlic } finely sliced.

Lightly fry the onions and garlic in the ghee or other fat. Then add to it all the above curry ingredients except the meat and Dhall. Cook for 3 or 4 minutes. Add the meat, mix, cover the pan and cook slowly for about 30 minutes. Then add the Dhall, which should be ready, boiled in sufficient water to the consistency of a purée, and continue the cooking until the meat is tender. Salt to taste.

Meat and Potato Curry (Ghosht Aur Aloo)

450 g (1 lb) of beef or mutton cut up in convenient pieces.
450 g (1 lb) of small potatoes, quartered.
56 g (2 ozs) of ghee or other fat.
1 onion
1 clove of garlic } finely chopped.
1 tablespoonful of curry powder.
1 dessertspoonful of tomato purée or paste.
Salt.

Fry lightly in the ghee or other fat for 3 or 4 minutes the onions, garlic, then the curry powder. Continue the slow cooking for 2 or 3 minutes longer, adding gradually the tomato paste or purée. Add the meat and 285 ml (½ pint) of water. Mix well, cover the pan closely, and simmer gently for 30 minutes. Then add the potatoes and cook until done. Salt and lemon juice to taste.

A Cold Meat Curry (Ghosht Ka Salun)

450 g (1 lb) of cold meat (any kind), cut up into convenient pieces.

56 g (2 ozs) of ghee, butter, oil or any other kind of fat.

2 tablespoonfuls of finely minced onions.

½ teaspoonful of finely minced garlic.

1 heaped tablespoonful of ground corianders.

1 teaspoonful of ground turmeric.

½ teaspoonful of ground ginger.

½ teaspoonful of ground cummin seed.

½ teaspoonful of ground mustard seed.

½ teaspoonful of ground red chillies.

½ a teacupful of cocoanut milk.

Salt to taste.

Cook the onions and garlic for 2 or 3 minutes in the ghee or other fat, but do not let them brown. Then add all the other ingredients, except the meat and cocoanut milk. Stir well, cook on a slow fire for another 5 minutes or so. Add the meat and gradually a little stock or water to form a thickish gravy. Lastly add the cocoanut milk, a squeeze of lemon juice and salt to taste.

Methee Bhaji Curry

(Fresh Meat)

450 g (1 lb) of mutton, cut up into convenient pieces.

56 g (2 ozs) of ghee or other fat.

1 large onion ⎫
1 clove of garlic ⎭ finely minced.

1 heaped tablespoonful of curry powder.

1 dessertspoonful of tomato paste or 2 or 3 fresh tomatoes chopped finely.

2 handfuls of picked Methee leaves.

Salt and lemon juice to taste.

Fry lightly for 3 or 4 minutes in the ghee or other fat the onions and garlic, then add the curry powder. Cook for a minute or two, add the tomato paste and meat. Mix well, cover the pan and cook on a slow fire for 15 minutes. Then add the Methee leaves and continue the cooking until the meat is tender. If necessary add a little stock or water whilst the curry is cooking to form a thickish gravy.

This curry is usually served almost dry. Salt and lemon juice to taste. In lieu of the Methee leaves, use finely shredded spring greens or turnip tops and add to the curry powder ½ a teaspoonful of ground fenugreek (Methee).

Methee Bajee Curry

(Cooked Meat)

Make this curry in the same way as the fresh meat curry, but as the meat is already cooked, the Methee Bajee must be cooked in the curry ingredients before the meat is added, for the meat will only need simmering until warmed through. A tablespoonful of thick cocoanut milk is usually added.

In lieu of the Methee Bajee, use finely shredded spring greens, turnip tops or broccoli and add ½ teaspoonful of ground fenugreek (Methee).

Minced Meat and Lettuce Curry
(Kheema Aur Bhagi)

225 g (½ lb) of finely minced cooked meat of any kind freed from skin and fat is curried as follows:

1 small onion } finely minced and lightly fried in
1 clove of garlic } a little ghee or other fat.

and then the following ingredients are added:

1 dessertspoonful of ground corianders.
1 teaspoonful of ground turmeric.
½ teaspoonful of ground chillies.
½ teaspoonful of ground ginger.
½ teaspoonful of ground cummin seed.
¼ teaspoonful of ground fenugreek.

Mix thoroughly and continue the cooking for 2 or 3 minutes longer. Then add a small sized lettuce, coarsely shredded. Simmer for 10 minutes or so, add the meat and salt to taste and when the meat is warmed through the curry is ready.

Mince Curry (*Kheema*)

In 56 g (2 ozs) of ghee or other fat lightly fry for 2 or 3 minutes:

1 large onion
2 cloves of garlic $\Big\}$ very finely minced.

Then add:

1 tablespoonful of curry powder.
1 teaspoonful of tomato purée (or 2 or 3 fresh tomatoes, chopped finely).

Mix and continue the frying for a minute or two longer. Now add 450 g (1 lb) of finely minced fresh lean beef or mutton and a tablespoonful of sour curds. Salt to taste. Mix thoroughly and cook slowly until done.

This curry should not be quite dry, neither should it have any gravy.

Egg, Liver and Tripe Curries

Madras Egg Curry

Six hard-boiled eggs cut lengthwise in halves.

In 56 g (2 ozs) of ghee or other fat, fry lightly for 2 or 3 minutes 2 tablespoonfuls of chopped onions and 1 clove of garlic, finely sliced. Add 1 heaped tablespoonful of curry powder. Stir thoroughly, and continue the frying for 2 or 3 minutes longer. Add a teaspoonful of tomato paste or 225 g ($\frac{1}{2}$ lb) of fresh ripe tomatoes, finely chopped, and sufficient water to form a thickish gravy. Salt and lemon juice to taste and simmer for 5 to 10 minutes. Then add the eggs and warm through.

Madras Egg Curry

(Fish Flavour)

Six hard-boiled eggs cut lengthwise in halves.

In 56 g (2 ozs) of ghee or other fat, fry lightly a large onion and a clove of garlic, both very finely sliced. Add to this a tablespoonful of curry powder or a heaped dessertspoonful of curry paste. Mix well and continue the frying for another minute or two. Then add a piece of salt fish about 50 mm (2 inches) square and 285 ml ($\frac{1}{2}$ pint) of thick cocoanut milk.

Simmer with the pan uncovered until it forms a thick rich gravy. Remove the fish. Salt and lemon juice to taste. Add the eggs and let them warm through.

A variation of the above curry can be had by adding a dessertspoonful of tomato paste to the curry ingredients.

Egg Curry (Undah Ka Salun)

Fry lightly in a saucepan in a tablespoonful of ghee or other fat, 1 onion and 1 clove of garlic, finely minced. Add to this:

1 dessertspoonful of ground corianders.
1 teaspoonful of ground turmeric.
½ teaspoooful of ground ginger.
½ teaspoonful of ground chillies.
½ teaspoonful of ground cummin seed.

Mix and add to it 570 ml (1 pint) of thin cocoanut milk and simmer until it begins to thicken. Then add 6 hard-boiled eggs, cut lengthwise in halves, and 2 tablespoonfuls of thick cocoanut milk. Salt and lemon juice to taste.

Egg Curry with Brinjals

This curry is made as an ordinary egg curry (above) except that when the sauce is ready, and before the eggs are added to it, the uncooked brinjals, cut up into convenient pieces, are cooked in the sauce.

Egg Curry with Green Peas

This is made in the same way as Egg Curry with brinjals (see above), but the peas must be quite cooked before being added to the sauce.

Liver Curry

450 g (1 lb) of liver, well washed and cut up into convenient pieces.

Fry lightly in a dessertspoonful of ghee or other fat for 3 or 4 minutes: a small onion and a clove of garlic, sliced finely.
Then add:

2 tablespoonfuls of ground corianders.
A heaped teaspoonful of ground turmeric.
½ teaspoonful of ground cummin seed.
½ teaspoonful of ground mustard seed.
½ teaspoonful of ground chillies.

Mix well and cook for another 4 or 5 minutes on a slow fire. Add the liver and a very little water. Simmer for 10 minutes, then add a tablespoonful of finely scraped cocoanut or a dessert-spoonful of finely desiccated cocoanut.

Continue the simmering and add salt and lemon juice to taste.

Madras Liver Curry

450 g (1 lb) of sheep's liver cut into 25 mm (1 inch) cubes.
1 onion and a clove of garlic finely sliced.
56 g (2 ozs) of ghee or oil.
1 tablespoonful of curry powder or curry paste.
1 dessertspoonful of tamarind pulp.
Salt to taste.

Fry lightly in the ghee or oil for 3 or 4 minutes the onions and garlic. Add the curry powder or paste and continue the frying for 2 or 3 minutes, then add the tomato paste. Mix well and thin it down with water to a thickish gravy. Add the liver and simmer until cooked. Add the tarmarind pulp and salt to taste.

Dry Tripe Curry

450 g (1 lb) of tripe, well washed and cut into 50 mm (2 inch) lengths as thick as macaroni, just enough water to cover it, and simmer gently until cooked. Then drain thoroughly.

In a *sauté* pan fry lightly for 2 or 3 minutes in just enough oil: 1 onion sliced, 2 fresh or pickled chillies, cut lengthwise in halves, and ½ teaspoonful of finely chopped fresh or pickled ginger. Add to this a dessertspoonful of curry paste and a tablespoonful of freshly scraped cocoanut. Mix well, toss into it the tripe, and let it warm through thoroughly.

If there is any gravy, it must be absorbed by adding a little more scraped cocoanut. Salt and lemon juice to taste.

Tripe Curry

450 g (1 lb) of tripe, well washed and cut up into convenient pieces, just covered with cold water and simmered until tender. Make a paste with a little vinegar of the following ingredients:

2 dessertspoonfuls of ground corianders.
A heaped teaspoonful of ground turmeric.
A generous pinch of ground cummin seed.
½ teaspoonful of ground mustard seed.
½ teaspoonful of ground pepper.

In a dessertspoonful of ghee or other fat, fry lightly for 3 or 4 minutes a large onion, a clove of garlic, finely sliced, and 2 or 3 red dry chillies, cut lengthwise and the inner seeds removed.

When the onions begin to brown, add the paste made as above. Mix thoroughly and cook on a slow fire for 3 or 4 minutes. Then add gradually 285 ml ($\frac{1}{2}$ pint) of cocoanut milk and, stirring all the time, the cooked tripe and as much of the stock as will make a thickish gravy. Salt to taste and about a teaspoonful of tamarind pulp.

X

Dry Curries — Bhoona Ghosht

THESE curries excel in Southern India and are made both from fresh meat and (amongst the English and Anglo-Indians) cold cooked meat. They are usually served with the different kinds of pepper water or Mulligatawny.

Devilled Poultry

Use the jointed legs of fowl, duck, goose, turkey, wild fowl, etc. Score them and rub well into them a paste, made with vinegar or tamarind pulp and the following ingredients:

    1 dessertspoonful of ground turmeric.
    1 teaspoonful of ground chillies.
    ¼ teaspoonful of ground black pepper.

Fry in ghee or other fat. Salt to taste. Drain and serve.

Chicken (Moorgee) Country Captain

A jointed chicken, fried in a little fat until a light brown. Remove it, and, in the fat, fry 6 slices of green ginger, 1 onion sliced up finely, 3 or 4 red or green chillies cut lengthwise, and a generous pinch of black pepper.

Add the chicken and just sufficient water for it to cook in until tender. Salt to taste.

Chicken (Moorgee) Country Captain

(Another way)

    1 chicken jointed in convenient pieces.
    56 g (2 ozs) of ghee or other fat.
    2 tablespoonfuls of chopped onions.
    1 clove of garlic, sliced finely.
    ½ teaspoonful of ground chillies.
    ½ teaspoonful of ground turmeric.

Fry the onions and garlic in ghee or other fat, add the ground chillies and turmeric. Cook for 2 or 3 minutes, then fry the pieces of chicken in it, adding more ghee if necessary. Add a sufficiency of water to form a thick gravy and simmer gently until the chicken is cooked. Salt and lemon juice to taste.

Serve garnished with crisply fried onions.

Chicken (Moorgee) Country Captain

(Another way)

One chicken jointed up and slowly simmered in a little water until almost cooked.

Fry in some fat for 4 or 5 minutes a small onion, finely sliced. Then add to it 2 or 3 green chillies, 6 thin slices of green ginger and a little pepper. Add the chicken, but not the gravy and let the chicken brown in the fat with the other ingredients for about 15 minutes. Then add a little of the chicken stock. Simmer until the meat is quite tender. Salt to taste and serve.

Country Captain of Cold Meat

450 g (1 lb) of cold meat of any sort cut up in convenient pieces is added to a pan in which:

2 sliced onions.
2 or 3 fresh or pickled chillies chopped finely.
1 teaspoonful of ground turmeric.
1 saltspoonful of ground black pepper.
½ teaspoonful of ground ginger.

have been cooked for 3 or 4 minutes.

The meat is then fried in this mixture until browned, but not hardened. Salt and lemon juice to taste.

Cold chicken or game of any sort is utilized in a like manner.

Madras Dry Curry of Fresh Meat

Cut up 450 g (1 lb) of lean beef or mutton into 12 mm (½ inch) cubes.

Using a deep *sauté* pan, melt in it a heaped tablespoonful of fat and then add a tablespoonful of chopped onions, ¼ of a small teaspoonful of chopped garlic and ½ teaspoonful of ground ginger.

Half cook these ingredients and then add a tablespoonful of

curry powder or preferably curry paste. Stir thoroughly and cook on a slow fire for 2 or 3 minutes longer.

Add the meat and mix the whole lightly but thoroughly, cover the pan closely and cook on a slow fire until the meat is tender.

This curry must be watched carefully to see that it does not stick to the pan. If, when the meat is tender, there is still gravy in the pan, it must be absorbed by adding a sprinkling of desiccated cocoanut. Salt to taste and a squeeze of lemon juice at the finish.

Madras Dry Curry of Cold Cooked Meat

Cut 450 g (1 lb) of meat into 12 mm ($\frac{1}{2}$ inch) cubes and sprinkle over it:

> 1 heaped teaspoonful of ground turmeric.
> $\frac{1}{2}$ teaspoonful of ground chillies.
> $\frac{1}{2}$ teaspoonful of ground pepper.
> $\frac{1}{2}$ teaspoonful of ground mustard seed.
> 1 saltspoonful of ground fenugreek.

Add a tablespoonful of tamarind juice and mix the whole lightly and thoroughly.

In a *sauté* pan, put in a heaped tablespoonful of fat, a tablespoonful of chopped onions, $\frac{1}{2}$ teaspoonful of chopped garlic. Half cook the garlic and onions, then add the marinade as above. Cook slowly, stirring occasionally until the meat is thoroughly warmed through, and all moisture absorbed. Salt to taste.

Dry Curry (Bhoona Ghosht)

> 450 g (1 lb) of mutton or lamb freed from fat and skin, and cut into 25 mm (1 inch) squares.
> 1 tablespoonful of ghee or other fat.
> 1 tablespoonful of finely minced onions.
> 2 cloves of garlic very finely sliced lengthwise.
> 1 or 2 fresh or pickled chillies, cut in halves lengthwise.
> 1 tablespoonful of curry powder.
> 1 dessertspoonful of vinegar.
> 1 tablespoonful of desiccated cocoanut (very fine cut).
> Salt to taste.

Fry lightly in the ghee or other fat, the onions, garlic and chillies for a couple of minutes, then add the curry powder. Mix well, and cook on a slow fire for another minute or two.

Now add the meat and vinegar, stir thoroughly, cover the pan, and cook on a moderate fire, stirring it every now and again until the meat is tender. Watch carefully to see that the meat does not burn. Add salt to taste, then the cocoanut which will absorb all the fat and meat juice (if any).

Dry Curry of Cold Meat (*Chundole*)

(A Moglai Dish)

Cut up 450 g (1 lb) of cooked mutton or beef into 12 mm (½ inch) cubes – preferably underdone meat.

Using a *sauté* pan, warm in it a tablespoonful of ghee or other fat and add:

> 2 tablespoonfuls of chopped onion.
> About ½ teaspoonful or rather less of finely chopped garlic.
> 3 fresh or pickled chillies, cut lengthwise in halves.
> ½ teaspoonful of finely chopped fresh or pickled ginger.

Cook until the onions are half cooked, but do not brown them. Now add 1 heaped teaspoonful of ground turmeric and ¼ teaspoonful of ground red chillies. Mix well, cook slowly for 2 or 3 minutes and then add the meat. Stir the whole lightly and cook until the meat is warmed right through. Salt and lemon juice to taste.

Dry Mince Curry (*Bhoona Kheema*)

> 450 g (1 lb) minced mutton or beef.
> 1 large onion ⎫
> 2 cloves of garlic ⎬ finely minced.
> 1 tablespoonful of curry powder.
> 1 dessertspoonful of tomato paste.
> 2 ordinary cloves.
> 2 cardamoms.
> A 50 mm (2 inch) stick of cinnamon.
> 56 g (2 ozs) of ghee or other fat.
> Lemon juice and salt to taste.

Fry lightly in the ghee or other fat for 3 or 4 minutes the onions, garlic, cloves, cardamoms, and cinnamon. Then add the curry powder, and mixing well, blend in with it the tomato paste, and after 3 or 4 minutes' slow cooking, add the meat. Mix thoroughly, cover the pan and cook slowly without adding any moisture for half and hour or so, when the meat will be cooked. Salt and lemon juice to taste.

This curry must cook in its own juice and any excess of moisture in it must be absorbed by the addition of a dessertspoonful of desiccated cocoanut. The curry is usually so dry that it is almost granular.

Dry Curry of Cooked Meat

Cut the meat up into convenient pieces.

In a frying pan with a little ghee or other fat, fry lightly for 2 or 3 minutes, sufficient cocoanut paste and twice its bulk of curry powder. Toss the meat into the mixture and let it warm through.

Vindaloos

In Southern India where the curries are as a rule much hotter than those in other parts of India, Vindaloos take the lead.

Rich meats are chosen for this dish, such as fat pork, fat ducks and geese. The curry ingredients are varied and if ground on a curry stone the liquid used for moistening them is vinegar. If the ingredients are already in a powder form they are mixed into a paste with vinegar.

Vindaloos are hot, and it is therefore customary to use more chillies than in ordinary curries. A dry preparation known as Vindaloo mixture when mixed into a paste with vinegar gives perfect results and saves a great amount of time and trouble.

Pork Vindaloo (Punny Vindaloo)

450 g (1 lb) of fat pork cut up into convenient sizes.
2 heaped tablespoonfuls of chopped onions.
½ a small teaspoonful of chopped garlic.
2 tablespoonfuls of vindaloo mixture, mixed into a paste with vinegar.
56 g (2 ozs) of ghee or any other fat.
Salt to taste.

Put the ghee or fat into a stewpan together with the chopped onions and garlic. Cook until the onions begin to change colour, then add the vindaloo paste. Stir well and cook for 2 or 3 minutes on a slow fire, taking care that it does not catch or burn.

Now add the pork. Mix the whole thoroughly well, cover the pan closely and cook on a slow fire until tender. This dish wants watching, and when necessary a little water is added to form a thick rich gravy. Salt to taste.

Pork Vindaloo (Punny Vindaloo)

(Another way)

Make a pickle of the following:

1 medium-sized onion and 2 or 3 cloves of garlic, finely
    sliced.
2 tablespoonfuls of ground corianders.
1 dessertspoonful of ground turmeric.
1 teaspoonful of ground cummin seed.
1 teaspoonful of ground chillies.
1 teaspoonful of ground ginger.
1 teaspoonful of ground mustard seed.
1 saltspoonful of ground fenugreek.
1 saltspoonful of ground pepper.

With a tablespoonful or more of vinegar, and a tablespoonful
of thick tarmarind pulp made with vinegar. Add to it 450 g (1 lb)
of fat pork cut up in convenient pieces. Stand aside for 24 hours.

To cook: Turn this pickled meat and whatever liquor there may
be in it into a roomy saucepan containing rather more ghee
or other fat than usual. Cover the pan closely and simmer until
the meat is cooked. Salt to taste.

This dish must be very rich and hot to be perfect.

Duck Vindaloo (Vathoo Vindaloo)

1 fat duck jointed up.
56 g (2 ozs) of ghee or other fat.
1 large onion, chopped finely.
6 thin slices of garlic.
2 tablespoonfuls of vindaloo mixture made into a paste with
    vinegar.
2 red chillies, cut lengthwise in halves and the inner seeds
    removed.
Salt.

Fry the onions and garlic in the fat, but do not brown them.
Add the vindaloo paste and chillies. Stir thoroughly and cook
on a slow fire for 3 or 4 minutes. Then add the duck and a little
water. Mix well and cover the pan closely. Simmer until
thoroughly cooked. Salt to taste.

This curry must be rich and hot.

Young fat geese (Perri Vathoo) are also curried in the same
manner.

Duck Vindaloo (Vathoo Vindaloo)

(Another way)

1 duck jointed.

56 g (2 ozs) of ghee or other fat.

A large onion and 2 cloves of garlic, finely sliced.

2 or 3 red chillies, cut lengthwise, and the inner seeds removed.

3 dessertspoonfuls of ground corianders
1 heaped teaspoonful of ground turmeric
½ teaspoonful of ground ginger
½ teaspoonful of ground cummin seed   } blend into a paste with vinegar.
½ teaspoonful of ground black pepper
½ teaspoonful of ground chillies
1 saltspoonful of ground fenugreek

Fry lightly in the fat, the onions, garlic and dry chillies. Then add the curry paste and cook on a slow fire for 3 or 4 minutes.

Add the duck. Mix well and let it fry in the curry ingredients for a few minutes longer. Add sufficient water to form a thickish gravy. Cover the pan closely and continue the simmering until the duck is tender. Salt to taste.

Young fat geese (Perri Vathoo) are also curried in the same way.

Beef Vindaloo (Madoo Vindaloo)

450 g (1 lb) of beef cut up into fairly large pieces.

Mix into a paste with vinegar:

1 dessertspoonful of ground corianders.
½ teaspoonful of ground cummin seed.
1 teaspoonful of ground turmeric.
½ teaspoonful of ground mustard seed.
½ teaspoonful of ground chillies.
1 saltspoonful of ground black pepper.
1 saltspoonful of ground ginger.

In 56 g (2 ozs) of ghee or other fat lightly fry for 3 or 4 minutes:

1 large onion
2 cloves of garlic   } finely sliced.
2 fresh or pickled green chillies finely minced.

Add the above paste and cook for 3 or 4 minutes longer, then add the meat, and with the pan covered let it cook in its own juice as long as possible. When necessary add just enough water to form a thick rich gravy. Salt and lemon juice to taste.

Beef Vindaloo (Madoo Vindaloo)

(Another way)

450 g (1 lb) of fat beef cut up in convenient pieces.

56 g (2 ozs) of ghee or other fat.

2 heaped tablespoonfuls of finely chopped onions.

1 teaspoonful of finely chopped garlic.

2 tablespoonfuls of vindaloo mixture made into a paste with vinegar.

2 dry red chillies, cut lengthwise in halves and the inner seeds removed.

Salt.

In the ghee or other fat fry lightly for 2 or 3 minutes the onions, garlic and chillies. Add the vindaloo paste. Mix well and cook on a slow fire for a further 3 or 4 minutes.

Add the meat and a very little water. Mix the whole thoroughly well, cover the pan closely and simmer until tender. Salt to taste.

Beef Vindaloo (Madoo Vindaloo)

(Another way)

450 g (1 lb) of beef cut up as desired.

With a sufficiency of vinegar make a thickish paste of the following ingredients:

1 medium-sized onion ⎫
2 or more cloves of garlic ⎬ very finely minced.

2 tablespoonfuls of ground corianders.

1 dessertspoonful of ground turmeric.

1 teaspoonful of ground cummin seed.

1 teaspoonful of ground ginger.

1 teaspoonful of ground red chillies.

½ teaspoonful of ground mustard seed.

¼ teaspoonful of ground fenugreek.

Thoroughly mix the meat in it and stand aside for 4 or more hours – the longer the better.

In a roomy stewpan warm 2 tablespoonfuls of ghee or other fat and then add the meat and all the mixture in which it is standing as well as 285 ml ($\frac{1}{2}$ pint) of water. Cover the pan closely and simmer gently until cooked. Salt to taste.

Fish—Muchlee—Meen

THE usual method of cooking fish in India is to curry it, and even when fried it is flavoured with certain curry ingredients. Different kinds of fish are utilized, the principal ones being Pomfret and Seer. In England, however, these Indian fish dishes are best produced by using such fish as mackerel, eels, hake, cod, fresh herring, halibut, turbot, etc., and of these the very best is mackerel in season.

Fish Curry

Fry lightly in 56 g (2 ozs) of oil or other fat 2 tablespoonfuls of chopped onions and 1 clove of garlic, very finely sliced. Now add 1 heaped dessertspoonful of curry powder or curry paste. Stir well and cook slowly for 3 or 4 minutes. Then add 1 dessertspoonful of tomato paste or 225 g ($\frac{1}{2}$ lb) of fresh tomatoes chopped up. Stir and cook for another 4 or 5 minutes and then convert it into a thickish sauce by adding water gradually, and let it come to the boil. Fillets or slices of fish can now be placed in the sauce and allowed to cook slowly until done. Salt and lemon juice to taste.

After the fish is in the sauce it must not be stirred, but to prevent it from sticking to the bottom of the pan, the pan must be moved gently backwards and forwards.

Fish Curry

(Another way)

With a little tamarind juice or vinegar blend together the following ingredients:

1 tablespoonful of ground corianders.
1 teaspoonful of ground turmeric.
1 teaspoonful of ground cummin seed.
$\frac{1}{2}$ teaspoonful of ground ginger.
$\frac{1}{2}$ teaspoonful of ground red chillies.
$\frac{1}{2}$ teaspoonful of ground fenugreek.

Fry in 2 or 3 tablespoonfuls of either mustard oil, gingili oil, olive oil or any other fat 2 small onions and 2 or 3 cloves of garlic, sliced finely, then add the above curry mixture and cook for another 5 minutes. Add sufficient cocoanut milk to make a thickish gravy. Salt to taste. Add whatever kind of fish you have to the sauce, keep the pan uncovered, and simmer gently until the fish is cooked. Shake the pan occasionally to prevent the fish sticking to the pan.

Bombay Fish Curry

A sufficiency of fresh fish of any kind – whole, sliced or filleted.
56 g (2 ozs) of ghee or butter or oil.
1 tablespoonful of chopped onion.
A clove of garlic, finely minced.
2 dried red chillies, cut lengthwise with the inner seeds removed.
1 level dessertspoonful of ground corianders.
1 level teaspoonful of ground turmeric.
1 level teaspoonful of ground mustard seed.
$\frac{1}{4}$ teaspoonful of ground chillies.
$\frac{1}{2}$ teaspoonful of chopped fresh or pickled green ginger.
Cocoanut milk.

Lightly cook in the fat for 2 or 3 minutes the onions, garlic, ginger, chillies and ground spices, Add 285 ml ($\frac{1}{2}$ pint) of thin cocoanut milk in which a teaspoonful of rice flour has been mixed. Salt and lemon juice to taste. Cook on a slow fire, and when it thickens add the fish, and when this is cooked add 2 tablespoonfuls of thick cocoanut milk.

After adding the curry the fish must not be stirred, but the pan shaken every now and again to prevent sticking.

Eel Curry (Muchlee Curry)

Eels cut up in 50 mm (2 inch) lengths.
56 g (2 ozs) of ghee or other fat.
1 large onion　　⎫
1 clove of garlic　⎬　finely sliced.
1 tablespoonful of curry powder.
1 dessertspoonful of tomato paste or 225 g ($\frac{1}{2}$ lb) of tomatoes, peeled and chopped finely.
Salt to taste.

Fry lightly in the ghee or other fat for 3 or 4 minutes the onion and garlic, then add the curry powder. Mix well and continue the slow cooking for another 2 or 3 minutes, gradually working into it the tomato paste or chopped tomatoes and sufficient water to form a thick gravy. Salt to taste. Then add the fish and, if liked, a little lemon juice or tamarind pulp. Simmer gently with the pan uncovered until the fish is cooked.

Do not stir this curry, but shake the pan occasionally.

Salt Fish and Tomato Curry

1 dessertspoonful of ground corianders.
1 teaspoonful of ground turmeric.
½ teaspoonful of ground cummin seed.
½ teaspoonful of ground red chillies.
6 slices of fresh green or pickled ginger.
1 large onion ⎫ sliced finely.
2 cloves of garlic ⎭

Fry lightly for 3 or 4 minutes the above ingredients in 2 table-spoonfuls of mustard, gingili or olive oil. Add to it 225 g (½ lb) of tomatoes with the skins removed and sufficient salt fish for the gravy formed. Simmer gently until the fish is cooked. For acidity add a dessertspoonful of tamarind juice, or rather less of vinegar. Salt to taste, and when the fish is cooked add 2 tablespoonfuls of thick cocoanut milk.

The above is sufficient for 6 Bombay Ducks cut across in halves.

Bombay Ducks or Other Salt Fish and Brinjals

Bombay Ducks cut in quarters and fried lightly in ghee or oil.
1 small brinjal cut lengthwise in half and then crosswise in slices 12 mm (½ inch) thick.
2 tablespoonfuls of fresh grated cocoanut or finely desiccated cocoanut.
1 large onion.
2 cloves of garlic.
1 tablespoonful of ground corianders.
1 teaspoonful of ground turmeric.
½ teaspoonful of ground cummin seed.
½ teaspoonful or less of ground red chillies.

In 2 tablespoonfuls of oil fry lightly the onions and garlic. Add all the other curry ingredients, except the cocoanut, and cook for another 5 minutes. Then add the brinjal. Mix lightly. Add 285 ml (½ pint) of water and salt to taste. Simmer gently until the brinjal is cooked and then add the fish. Simmer a little longer and just before serving add the grated cocoanut and a squeeze of lemon juice.

XIII

Prawns

FRESH prawns in India are very plentiful in the large seaport towns. The catches are so large that the surplus is usually salted and dried. They vary in size, some being quite tiny like shrimps, and others almost as large as small crayfish.

When the dried prawns are used they are soaked in cold water, wiped dry and then used. The smaller ones are as a rule curried, and the larger ones rubbed over with ground turmeric and ground chillies fried in oil, and eaten with Dhall and rice or pepper water and rice.

The recipes for the various prawn dishes are meant for the ordinary fresh cooked prawns, bottled or canned, as dried prawns are probably unobtainable.

Madras Prawn Curry

For this purpose use the ordinary cooked prawns.

Make a sauce by putting into your pan a tablespoonful of ghee or other fat, 2 tablespoonfuls of finely chopped onions and 1 or 2 cloves of garlic, also finely chopped. Cook the onions and garlic until they begin to change colour, then add either a tablespoonful of curry powder or curry paste (the latter will make a richer curry).

Stir well and let these ingredients fry for 3 or 4 minutes, then convert them into a thick sauce by adding 225 g ($\frac{1}{2}$ lb) of fresh tomatoes freed from their skins and finely chopped, or a dessert-spoonful of tomato paste dissolved in 285 ml ($\frac{1}{2}$ pint) of water. Salt and lemon juice to taste, let the sauce simmer until a richness appears in the curry, then add the prawns to the sauce, let them just warm through. Do not boil or they will lose their flavour and fall to pieces.

The addition of 2 tablespoonfuls of thick cocoanut milk is an improvement.

Crab, lobster and crayfish may be curried in the same way.

Prawn Curry

With a little tamarind juice or vinegar make a mixture of the following ingredients:

> 1 tablespoonful of ground corianders.
> 1 teaspoonful of ground turmeric.
> ½ teaspoonful of ground mustard seed.
> ½ teaspoonful of ground cummin seed.
> Less than ½ teaspoonful of ground red chillies.

Fry for 2 or 3 minutes in ghee or butter a small onion and 2 small cloves of garlic chopped up finely, but do not let them brown. Add the curry mixture. Stir thoroughly and cook slowly for another 3 or 4 minutes. Now add 285 ml (½ pint) of thick cocoanut milk and salt to taste. Then add 12 to 18 prawns and let them warm through thoroughly. Keep the pan uncovered.

Crab, lobster and crayfish may be curried in the same way.

Madras Dry Prawn Curry

Make the curry paste or mixture as above, but instead of using tamarind juice or vinegar use thick cocoanut milk. Fry in ghee or butter a small onion and 2 cloves of garlic, chopped up finely. Cook for 2 or 3 minutes, then add the curry paste and fry on a slow fire for a further 4 or 5 minutes. Now add 12 to 18 prawns and a tablespoonful of thick cocoanut milk. Salt to taste. Stir lightly until the prawns are warmed through and all moisture is absorbed. Serve with a little finely grated or desiccated cocoanut sprinkled over it.

Crab, lobster and crayfish may be curried in the same way.

Dry Prawn or Lobster Curry

> 12 to 18 prawns or 1 tin of lobster.
> 1 tablespoonful of ground corianders.
> 1 small teaspoonful of ground turmeric.
> ½ teaspoonful of ground cummin seed.
> ½ teaspoonful of ground ginger or 6 thin slices of fresh green or pickled ginger.
> 1 dessertspoonful of tamarind pulp.
> 1 onion ⎫
> 1 clove of garlic ⎬ finely minced.

Fry lightly in sufficient ghee or other fat for 3 or 4 minutes the onions and garlic, then add all the other ingredients except the prawns or lobster. Continue the frying for another 3 or 4 minutes, then stir in a dessertspoonful of tamarind pulp and with very little water make a thick gravy. Add the prawns or lobster, salt to taste and simmer until nearly dry.

Crab or crayfish may be curried in the same way.

Prawn or Lobster and Cucumber Curry

12 to 18 prawns or 1 fresh lobster or 1 tin of lobster.
12 12 mm ($\frac{1}{2}$ inch) slices of cucumber.
1 dessertspoonful of ground corianders.
1 small teaspoonful of ground tumeric.
$\frac{1}{2}$ teaspoonful of ground cummin seed.
$\frac{1}{2}$ teaspoonful of ground ginger or 6 thin slices of fresh green
   or pickled ginger.
3 fresh or pickled chillies, cut lengthwise in halves.
1 onion, finely minced.
1 clove of garlic.
Thick and thin cocoanut milk.
Ghee or other fat.

Fry lightly in sufficient ghee or other fat for 3 or 4 minutes the onion, garlic and chillies, then stir into it all the other ingredients except the prawns or lobster and cucumber. Mix and continue the frying for another few minutes. Now add 285 ml ($\frac{1}{2}$ pint) of thin cocoanut milk and the cucumber and simmer until the cucumber is cooked, adding if necessary a little more thin cocoanut milk.

Add the prawns or lobster and 2 tablespoonfuls of thick cocoanut milk. Simmer for a few minutes with the pan uncovered. Salt to taste and serve. In lieu of the cucumber, pumpkin, brinjals and marrow cut up into convenient pieces can be used.

Crab or crayfish may be curried in the same way.

Prawn and Egg Curry

4 hard-boiled eggs cut lengthwise in halves.
12 prawns (cooked).
56 g (2 ozs) of ghee or other fat.
1 heaped tablespoonful of finely chopped onion.
1 or 2 cloves of garlic, finely minced.
2 fresh or pickled chillies, cut lengthwise.

1 tablespoonful of curry powder.
1 dessertspoonful of tomato paste.
Salt and lemon juice.
Thick cocoanut milk.

Fry lightly for 3 or 4 minutes in the ghee or other fat the onion, garlic and chillies, then add the curry powder or curry paste and the tomato paste. Stir thoroughly and continue this slow cooking for 2 or 3 minutes longer. Thin this mixture down into a thickish gravy by adding gradually a little water. Simmer gently. Salt and lemon juice to taste, and finally a little thick cocoanut milk. Then add the eggs and prawns.

The gravy must be thick and cling to the eggs.

Prawn and Brinjal Curry

12 prawns.
1 moderate-sized brinjal cut up into convenient pieces.
56 g (ozs) of ghee or other fat.
1 heaped tablespoonful of finely minced onion.
2 cloves of garlic finely minced.
2 fresh or pickled chillies, cut lengthwise.
1 tablespoonful of curry powder.
1 dessertspoonful of tomato paste.
Salt and lemon juice to taste.
Thick cocoanut milk.

Fry lightly for 2 or 3 minutes in the ghee or other fat the onion, garlic and chillies, then add the curry powder and the tomato paste. Stir thoroughly and continue the slow cooking for another 5 minutes.

Gradually convert this into a sauce with a little water, bring to the boil, add the brinjal, salt to taste and simmer until the brinjal is cooked. Add the prawns, 2 tablespoonfuls of thick cocoanut milk and a squeeze of lemon juice. The gravy of this curry must also be thick, so that in making the sauce for the brinjals bear this in mind.

Madras Prawn and Brinjal Curry

Fry lightly in 56 g (2 ozs) of ghee or other fat 2 tablespoonfuls of finely chopped onions and 1 or 2 cloves of garlic. Cook until they begin to change colour, then add either a heaped tablespoonful of curry powder or curry paste (the latter will make a richer gravy). Stir well and let these ingredients fry for 3 or 4 minutes, then convert them into a thickish sauce by adding 225 g ($\frac{1}{2}$ lb) of fresh tomatoes freed from their skins and finely chopped, or a dessertspoonful of tomato paste dissolved in 285 ml ($\frac{1}{2}$ pint) of water, and let the sauce simmer until a richness appears in the curry.

Have an aubergine cut up into convenient pieces, and add them to the sauce; cook slowly until quite tender. Then add 12 to 18 prawns and let them just warm through. Salt and lemon juice to taste. The addition of 2 tablespoonfuls of thick cocoanut milk is an improvement.

Molees

A MOLEE is essentially a Southern Indian, Ceylon or Malay dish, the basis being cocoanut milk. Molees may be made of different kinds of vegetables, hard-boiled eggs, fish, prawns, lobster, or a blend of any of these. As a rule, already cooked materials are used, but there are exceptions.

The most suitable vegetables for this dish, apart from the vegetables obtainable in the East, are: cooked green peas, potatoes, carrots, beans, cauliflower and cucumber. It is advisable to have a mixture of any two or three or all of these cut up in convenient sizes.

How to Prepare a Molee for General Use

Thick cocoanut milk.
Onions, finely sliced.
Garlic, finely sliced.
Fresh or pickled chillies, cut lengthwise.
Fresh green or pickled ginger, in thin slices.
Ground turmeric.
Ghee or butter.
Salt.

Lightly fry the onions and garlic in the ghee or butter and add to this the chillies, green ginger, and ground turmeric. Cocoanut milk is then added to make the sauce. Salt to taste.

Do not cover the pan at any time during the cooking, and bring to the boil very slowly as the cocoanut milk is liable to go oily.

Fish Molee (Meen Molee)

4 fillets or cutlets of fish.
56 g (2 ozs) of ghee or butter.
1 tablespoonful of finely chopped onions.
½ teaspoonful of finely chopped garlic.

½ dozen fresh green chillies, cut lengthwise in halves.
½ dozen thin slices of fresh or pickled green ginger.
½ teaspoonful of ground turmeric.
Thick cocoanut milk.
Salt.
4 cardamoms.
4 cloves.
A 50 mm (2 inch) stick of cinnamon.

Using a *sauté* pan, fry lightly in the ghee or butter the chopped onions, garlic, spices and sliced ginger. Cook, but do not brown the onions, then add the turmeric and green chillies, stir and simmer on a slow fire for 2 or 3 minutes. Add the cocoanut milk and salt to taste and gradually bring to boiling point. Then add the fillets or cutlets of fish, but do not stir. Simmer until the fish is done.

On no account stir this dish after the fish is added or it will be a pulp. The cocoanut milk must be thick.

Fish Molee of Cooked Fish (*Meen Molee*)

450 g (1 lb) of cold cooked fish (preferably fillets or cutlets).
56 g (2 ozs) of ghee or other fat.
570 ml (1 pint) of thick cocoanut milk.
1 small teaspoonful of ground turmeric.
2 tablespoonfuls of finely chopped onions.
½ teaspoonful of garlic finely sliced.
½ teaspoonful of fresh or pickled green ginger, finely sliced.
6 red or green chillies (preferably fresh) cut lengthwise in halves.
Salt.

Using a moderately deep *sauté* pan, cook in the ghee or other fat the onions, garlic, ginger and chillies, but do not let them brown. Add the turmeric and cook the mixture on a slow fire for 3 or 4 minutes longer, then add the cocoanut milk, salt to taste, and simmer gently.

Lastly place the fish in the sauce, warm through thoroughly, but do not let the fish break up.

Prawn or Lobster Molees

Prawns or lobster.
56 g (2 ozs) of ghee or butter.
A large thinly sliced onion.

1 clove of garlic, finely minced.

$\frac{1}{2}$ teaspoonful of ground turmeric.

4 or 5 thin slices of green or pickled ginger.

3 fresh green or 2 dried red chillies cut lengthwise in halves
   and the inner seeds removed.

285 ml ($\frac{1}{2}$ pint) of thick cocoanut milk.

Salt.

Lightly fry the onions and garlic in the ghee or butter, add the
turmeric and ginger, then gradually the cocoanut milk, finally
the chillies. Stir, and simmer for 10 minutes. Salt to taste. Then
add as much cooked prawns or lobster as is necessary for the
amount of sauce. The pan must not be covered during the cooking

Chicken Molee (Khoiee Molee)

Cold cooked chicken, freed from skin and bone.

1 large onion ⎫
1 clove of garlic ⎭ thinly sliced.

1 teaspoonful of ground turmeric.

6 thin slices of fresh green or pickled ginger.

3 or 4 fresh or dried chillies, cut lengthwise and the inner
   seeds removed.

6 whole cardamoms.

6 cloves.

1 stick of cinnamon 50 mm (2 inches) long.

28 g (1 oz) of ghee or butter.

570 ml (1 pint) of thick cocoanut milk.

Salt.

Lightly fry in the ghee or butter the onions, garlic, chillies,
ginger and spices. Then add the ground turmeric, cook on a
slow fire for 3 or 4 minutes. Now add the cocoanut milk gradually
and salt to taste. Bring gently to the boil, add the cold chicken,
and let it warm through. On no account cover the pan or the
molee will become oily.

Mutton or Beef Molee (Ahtoo Molee – Madoo Molee)

450 g (1 lb) of beef or mutton cut up onto convenient pieces and
slowly stewed in just sufficient water until tender.

Fry lightly in a spoonful of fat:

1 onion ⎫
1 clove of garlic ⎭ finely sliced.

1 teaspoonful of ground turmeric.
½ teaspoonful of ground mustard seed.
6 thin slices of green ginger.
1 saltspoonful of ground fenugreek.
2 or 3 red chillies, fresh or dried, cut lengthwise and the
    inner seeds removed.

Cook these ingredients on a slow fire for 4 or 5 minutes.
Then add the stewed meat and, a teacupful of thick cocoanut
milk. Salt to taste. Simmer gently for 4 or 5 minutes.

Duck Molee (*Vathoo Molee*)

This is cold roast duck freed from bone and skin and warmed
slowly in a molee gravy made as follows:

In an ounce of ghee or butter fry lightly:
    1 onion
    1 clove of garlic   } very finely sliced.

Then add:

    1 teaspoonful of ground turmeric.
    3 or more fresh or pickled chillies, cut lengthwise in halves
        and 6 thin slices of fresh green or pickled ginger.

Continue the slow cooking for 2 or 3 minutes longer. Then add
570 ml (1 pint) or rather less of thick cocoanut milk. Simmer until
the gravy beings to thicken. Add the cold duck and let it warm-
through. Salt to taste just before serving.

Brinjal Molee (*Kutherakoi Molee*)

    2 brinjals.
    1 onion (medium-sized)
    1 clove of garlic   } very finely sliced.
    2 fresh green or red chillies or 3 pickled chillies cut lengthwise
        in halves.
    6 thin slices of green or pickled ginger.
    1 teaspoonful of ground turmeric.
    Ghee or butter.
    Cocoanut milk.

Cut the brinjals into fairly thin slices. Rub them on both sides with the ground turmeric and a little salt. Then fry (but do not brown) them in ghee or butter. Drain.

Into a saucepan put some fresh ghee or butter and fry in it the onions, garlic, chillies and ginger. Cook until the onions are fairly well done, but not brown, and then add about 285 ml (½ pint) of thick cocoanut milk. Warm through and add the cooked brinjals, a little more salt if necessary, and simmer until the sauce thickens. Serve slices of lemon with it.

Egg Molee

3 hard-boiled eggs, cut lengthwise in halves.

1 large onion ⎱
1 clove of garlic ⎰ thinly sliced.

½ teaspoonful of ground turmeric.

½ teaspoonful of finely chopped fresh green or pickled ginger.

3 or 4 fresh or dried chillies, cut lengthwise and the inner seeds removed.

1 stick of cinnamon, 50 mm (2 inches) long.

28 g (1 oz) of ghee or butter.

285 ml (½ pint) of thick cocoanut milk.

Lightly fry the onion, garlic, chillies, ginger and cinnamon in the ghee or butter, and then add the turmeric and cook for 2 or 3 minutes. Thick cocoanut milk and salt to taste is now added and the mixture simmered until the sauce is thick enough to pour over the eggs. Do not cover the pan.

XV

Legumes

Dhalls – Lentils

INDIAN Dhalls, owing to their large percentage of vitamins, are a very reliable food. The proportion of fat in them being small, it is essential that in preparing them this should be remembered. Ghee, Gingili oil, Mustard oil, or any other edible oil, is the fat generally used in India.

Quite apart from Indian dishes, these Dhalls could and should be utilized by Westerners who will soon recognize their efficacy and economic value.

The following Dhalls are those most generally used:

Chenna (Bengal Gram).
Moosa or Mussoor.
Moong.
Jowari.
Toor.
Urad or Ooduth or Ooloonthoo.
Purapoo (Dhalls of different kinds).
Motchakotay or Mochekoy.
Koolthee (Gram), etc., etc.

All these Dhalls should be procurable at leading stores.

Bengal Dhall (Lentils)

225 g (½ lb) of Dhall or Egyptian lentils boiled soft in 570 ml (1 pint) of water.
56 g (2 oz) of ghee or other fat.
1 onion and a clove of garlic chopped finely.
1 tablespoonful of ground corianders ⎫ mixed into a
1 teaspoonful of ground turmeric ⎪ stiff paste with
½ teaspoonful of ground cummin seed ⎬ a little tamarind
½ teaspoonful of ground chillies ⎪ water or weak
1 saltspoonful of ground fenugreek ⎭ vinegar.

Fry lightly in the ghee or other fat for 2 or 3 minutes the onion and garlic, then add the paste made as above and continue the frying for a few minutes longer.

Now add the cooked Dhall and all the liquor that there is in it. Salt to taste, and simmer for 10 minutes before serving.

Dhall Curry

225 g ($\frac{1}{2}$ lb) of Dhall or Egyptian lentils boiled in 570 ml 1 pint of water together with a small onion chopped up finely.

28 g (1 oz) of ghee or other fat.

1 or 2 cloves of garlic ⎱
1 small onion   ⎰ chopped.

2 red chillies (seeds removed).

2 cardamoms.

2 cloves.

A 50 mm (2 inch) stick of cinnamon.

1 tablespoonful of curry powder.

1 dessertspoonful of tomato paste.

Fry lightly in the ghee or other fat the onion, garlic and spices for 2 or 3 minutes. Add the curry powder, mix, continue the cooking for 3 or 4 minutes longer, then add the tomato paste and boiled Dhall. Salt and lemon juice to taste. Simmer for 10 minutes before serving.

This Dhall can be thick or thin, according to the amount of water in which the Dhall has been boiled. It can be slightly varied in flavour by adding to the curry mixture before the Dhall is added, a heaped teaspoonful of pepper water mixture.

Dhall Curry

(Another way)

Well wash and drain 225 g ($\frac{1}{2}$ lb) of Dhall or lentils and place in a stewpan with the following ingredients:

1 medium-sized onion, chopped finely.

2 or 3 dried chillies.

1 dessertspoonful of ghee or other fat.

1 teaspoonful of ground turmeric.

$\frac{1}{2}$ teaspoonful of ground cummin seed.

6 or 8 peppercorns.

And with sufficient water boil these ingredients thoroughly, but do not let the Dhall pulp.

In another pan fry lightly in a dessertspoonful of ghee or other fat, 2 or 3 cloves of garlic sliced lengthwise, 2 ordinary cloves, 2 whole cardamoms, and a 25 mm (1 inch) stick of cinnamon.

Now add the contents of the first pan to the second. Bring to the boil. Salt to taste and simmer for 5 to 10 minutes.

Mogul Dhall Curry (Kutta Dhall)

225 g (½ lb) of Moosa or any other kind of Dhall (lentils will do), well washed and soaked in cold water overnight. Pour off the water and set the Dhall to boil in about 1.1 l (1 quart) or more of cold water until sufficiently cooked.

Fry lightly in 1 tablespoonful of ghee or other fat:

2 tablespoonfuls of chopped onions.
1 or 2 cloves of garlic chopped finely.
2 cloves.
4 cardamoms.
A stick of cinnamon about 50 mm (2 inches) long.

When the onions are beginning to change colour, add a heaped dessertspoonful of curry powder, stir thoroughly, and let the ingredients cook slowly for 2 or 3 minutes longer. Now add the boiled Dhall and stir the whole carefully. Salt to taste.

The Dhall should be about the consistency of porridge. The addition of a tablespoonful of tomato paste to the Dhall when being boiled is a great improvement, both in colour and taste.

Dhall or Indian Lentil Curry (Deccan Style)

Well wash in cold water 225 g (½ lb) of Moosa or Mussoor Dhall, and then set to boil in cold water until tender, but not pulped.

Fry in 2 tablespoonfuls of ghee or other fat:

2 tablespoonfuls of chopped onions.
1 or 2 cloves of garlic chopped finely.
2 cloves.
4 cardamoms.
A 50 mm (2 inch) stick of cinnamon.

Cook, but do not brown the onions, then add a heaped table-spoonful of curry powder, stir and fry these ingredients for 2 or 3 minutes, add the boiled Dhall and let it boil up. Salt to taste.

A variation in taste and appearance is obtained by the addition of one or two fresh tomatoes chopped up finely and cooked with curry ingredients before the Dhall is added.

5 minutes before dishing up add 2 tablespoonfuls of thick cocoanut milk.

Moosa or Mussoor Dhall Curry

113 g (¼ lb) of Dhall, well washed, and set to boil in about 570 ml (1 pint) of cold water until soft. Then stir into it:

> ½ teaspoonful of ground turmeric.
> 1 saltspoonful of ground ginger.
> 1 saltspoonful of ground red chillies.
> A large pinch of ground cummin seed.

Cover the pan and let the curry simmer for a few minutes.

Fry in a separate pan, but do not brown, 1 tablespoonful of onion and ½ teaspoonful of garlic chopped very finely, in 1 tablespoonful of ghee or other fat. Add to this the contents of the first pan and a little thick cocoanut milk. Salt to taste.

Fried Dhall

> 113 g (¼ lb) of Dhall or Egyptian lentils, well washed and soaked for an hour or two in cold water.
> 2 tablespoonfuls of ghee or other fat.
> 1 tablespoonful of chopped onions.
> 2 cloves of garlic finely minced.
> ½ teaspoonful of ground chillies.
> ½ teaspoonful of ground turmeric.
> ½ teaspoonful of ground ginger.

Fry the onions and garlic in the fat and then add the other ingredients and the Dhall well drained, and fry thoroughly for 10 minutes. Then add sufficient water to cover it and simmer until the Dhall is quite soft and almost pulpy. Salt to taste.

Meeta Dhall

225 g (½ lb) of any kind of Dhall or
    Egyptian lentils
1 onion sliced
1 or 2 dry red chillies, cut lengthwise,
    and the inner seeds removed
6 mint leaves

⎫
boil in 1.1 l
(1 quart) of water
until the
Dhall is
soft.

Fry lightly for 2 or 3 minutes in 56 g (2 ozs) of ghee or other fat:

1 small onion
1 clove of garlic   ⎬ finely sliced.
2 cloves.
2 cardamoms.
A 50 mm (2 inch) stick of cinnamon.

Add the boiled Dhall, salt to taste, and simmer for 10 minutes.

Meeta Dhall

(Another Way)

225 g (½ lb) of any kind of Dhall or
    Egyptian lentils
1 sliced onion
1 or 2 green chillies cut lengthwise
6 thin slices of green ginger

⎫
boil in 1.1 l
(1 quart) of water
until the
Dhall is
soft.

Fry lightly for 3 or 4 minutes in 56 g (2 ozs) of ghee or other fat:

1 small onion
1 clove of garlic   ⎬ finely sliced.
1 teaspoonful of ground turmeric.

Add the boiled Dhall, salt to taste, and simmer for 10 minutes
before serving.

Meeta Dhall

(Another way)

225 g (½ lb) of any kind of Dhall or lentils well washed in cold
    water.
1 onion either chopped up or finely sliced.
1 clove of garlic finely sliced lengthwise.
2 dry chillies.

These 4 ingredients must be set to boil in 1.1 l (1 quart) of cold water until the Dhall or lentils are soft but not pulped.

Using a stewpan fry lightly in 56 g (2 ozs) of ghee or other fat:

1 onion ⎫
1 clove of garlic ⎬ finely minced.
4 ordinary cloves.
4 whole cardamoms.
A 50 mm (2 inch) stick of cinnamon.
½ dozen mint leaves.

Do not let the onions brown in the least.

Add the boiled Dhall. Salt to taste, and simmer for 10 minutes or so.

Dhall with Brinjals (*Dhall aur Byngun*)

225 g (½ lb) of Dhall or Egyptian lentils ⎫ parboiled in 1.1 l
1 onion sliced ⎬ (1 quart) of water.

Fry lightly for 2 or 3 minutes in 28 to 56 g (1 to 2 ozs) of ghee or other fat:

1 sliced onion.
1 clove of garlic (minced).
1 dry chilli (inner seeds removed).
2 cloves.

Add to it 1 tablespoonful of curry powder, a heaped teaspoonful of pepper water mixture and a dessertspoonful of tomato paste. Mix and continue the cooking for a few minutes longer, then add the water in which the Dhall has been boiled and the brinjals cut up in 25 mm (1 inch) cubes. When these are about half cooked, add the parboiled Dhall. Salt to taste, and simmer until both are cooked.

Dhall with Spinach (*Meeta Dhall aur Bhagi*)

225 g (½ lb) of Dhall or Egyptian lentils ⎫ boiled in 570 ml
3 handfuls of spinach ⎬ (1 pint) of water
6 whole spring onions ⎪ until the Dhall is
2 fresh or pickled chillies ⎭ soft.

Fry lightly in 56 g (2 ozs) of ghee or other fat for 2 or 3 minutes:

1 onion ⎫
1 clove of garlic ⎬ minced finely.

2 cloves.
2 cardamoms.
A 25 mm (1 inch) stick of cinnamon.
1 teaspoonful of ground turmeric.
½ teaspoonful of ground cummin seed.

Add the cooked Dhall and spinach. Salt to taste and simmer gently for 10 minutes before serving.

Dhall with Greens (Dhall aur Bhagi)

225 g (½ lb) of Dhall or Egyptian lentils.

A small onion and a red chilli (inner seeds removed). Boil these in 570 ml (1 pint) of water until the Dhall is half cooked, then a handful of shredded cabbage, lettuce or any greens is added to the Dhall and cooked until the Dhall is soft.

Fry lightly in 28 to 56 g (1 to 2 ozs) of ghee or other fat:

1 large onion
1 clove of garlic   } sliced finely.

Add to this a heaped tablespoonful of curry powder and a dessertspoonful of pepper water mixture. Continue the cooking for 2 or 3 minutes longer, then stir in a dessertspoonful of tomato paste or 2 or 3 chopped tomatoes, and lastly add the boiled Dhall and greens. Salt to taste and a squeeze of lemon juice. Simmer for 10 minutes or longer before serving.

This must be of the consistency of a thick porridge.

Dhall

225 g (½ lb) of Moosa Dhall or lentils well washed and drained.

2 large onions
2 cloves of garlic
12 mm (½ inch) piece of fresh or pickled ginger   } chopped
4 fresh or pickled chillies, *or*   finely.
4 dry red chillies cut lengthwise in halves and
   the inner seeds removed

1 teaspoonful of ground turmeric.
570 ml (1 pint) of thin cocoanut milk.
2 tablespoonfuls of thick cocoanut milk.
Salt to taste.

Fry lightly in 56 g (2 ozs) of ghee or other fat for 3 or 4 minutes all the above chopped ingredients and turmeric. Now add the Dhall and continue the frying for a few minutes longer. Then add enough thin cocoanut milk to cover the Dhall. If insufficient add water. Bring to the boil and simmer until the Dhall is thoroughly well cooked, then add salt to taste and the thick cocoanut milk.

Dhall Rissoles

113 g (¼ lb) of Moosa Dhall or Egyptian lentils, 1 finely minced onion, 1 finely minced clove of garlic, boiled in a little water to the consistency of stiff porridge, cooled and well blended with:

> 56 g (2 ozs) of breadcrumbs.
> ¼ teaspoonful of ground turmeric.
> A pinch of ground chillies.
> 1 egg.
> 1 tablespoonful of flour.
> Salt to taste.

Form into rissoles with floured hands and fry in boiling fat.

XVI

Vegetables and Vegetable Curries

THERE are not many places in India where English vegetables are obtainable, and consequently Indian vegetables are used with advantage.

Behndis (Ladies' Fingers), Bandekoi. Bygun (Brinjal or Aubergine), Drumstick, Pumpkins, Snake Gourd, Yams, Nolecoles, etc., are very much appreciated, even though merely cooked as an ordinary English vegetable.

In addition to these there are many varieities of greens, spoken of as Bajees or Keerays in general, and known under such names as Methe, Soi, Mooroongakoi, etc. These, however, are only cooked in the Indian way.

Vegetable Curry (Chitchkee)

The most suitable European vegetables for currying are peas, carrots, turnips, tomatoes, potatoes, scarlet runners, and other beans, etc., either singly or blended as desired. Such of the vegetables as need it should be cut up into convenient sizes and shapes, as, for instance, carrots, turnips and potatoes, into cubes and strips and so on.

All these vegetables should be well washed and drained.

To Curry Uncooked Vegetables

In a sufficiency of ghee or other fat fry lightly a thinly sliced onion and 1 or 2 cloves of garlic. Add a tablespoonful of ground corianders, 1 teaspoonful of ground turmeric, $\frac{1}{2}$ teaspoonful of ground chillies, $\frac{1}{2}$ teaspoonful of ground cummin seed, $\frac{1}{2}$ teaspoonful of ground ginger, $\frac{1}{2}$ teaspoonful of ground mustard seed, and a saltspoonful of ground fenugreek.

Mix and fry on a slow fire for 3 or 4 minutes, then add the vegetables, toss lightly and cook for a further 3 or 4 minutes. Add now sufficient water to just cover the vegetables. Simmer gently and stir occasionally until the vegetables are cooked. Salt to taste.

To Curry Cooked Vegetables

Make a macedoine in the usual way of cooked vegetables. The curry ingredients as above, after being cooked in the ghee or other fat, should be converted into a gravy by adding thickish cocoanut milk, which should be gradually brought to the boil with the pan uncovered. The vegetables should now be added with salt to taste and allowed to warm through thoroughly. The stirring of these curries must be carefully done to prevent pulping.

Dry Vegetables Curries

These are usually made with partially cooked vegetables, and finished in the curry ingredients that have been prepared and cooked as above, but with more ghee or other fat. Moisture of any sort should be avoided. When dished, sprinkle over it a little finely desiccated cocoanut or finely grated fresh cocoanut.

Vegetable Curry

(Beans and Potatoes)

225 g ($\frac{1}{2}$ lb) of beans (use scarlet runners), prepared and sliced in the ordinary way.

225 g ($\frac{1}{2}$ lb) of potatoes peeled and cut up in 25 mm (1 inch) cubes.

225 g ($\frac{1}{2}$ lb) of fresh tomatoes chopped finely, or 1 dessert-spoonful of tomato paste.

Fry lightly for 2 or 3 minutes in 56 g (2 ozs) of ghee or other fat 1 large onion and a clove of garlic, finely sliced. Then add a heaped tablespoonful of curry powder and continue the frying on a slow fire for another 3 or 4 minutes. Add the chopped tomatoes or the tomato paste. Mix well and, if necessary, add a little water to make a thick gravy. Add the beans and simmer until nearly done. Then add the potatoes (they will only take a few minutes to cook). Salt and lemon juice to taste.

Madras Vegetable Curry

Using rather more ghee or other fat, onions and garlic than for a meat curry, cook until the onions and garlic are partially done, then add a sufficiency of curry powder. Mix thoroughly and cook on a slow fire for 3 or 4 minutes. Now add 2 or 3 chopped tomatoes, mix thoroughly and cook for another minute or two, then add the parboiled vegetables together with a little of the water in which they were boiled. Stir lightly and bring to the boil then simmer gently until the vegetables are cooked. Salt to taste. A little thick cocoanut milk or ordinary milk added 2 or 3 minutes before serving is a great improvement.

Dry red chillies are frequently added to make these curries hot.

Mutchakotay

(Haricot or Butter Beans Curry)

Soak overnight in cold water 225 g ($\frac{1}{2}$ lb) of haricot or butter beans and, together with a sliced onion, boil until soft.

Fry lightly in 56 g (2 ozs) of ghee or other fat:

    1 onion, finely sliced.

Add:

    1 dessertspoonful of curry powder and 1 dessertspoonful of curry paste.

Mix thoroughly and continue the cooking for 2 or 3 minutes longer. Add the boiled beans, salt to taste and simmer for 10 minutes before serving. A squeeze of lemon juice is an improvement.

Meeta Mutchakotay

(Haricot or Butter Beans Curry)

Soak in cold water overnight 225 g ($\frac{1}{2}$ lb) of haricot or butter beans and, together with a sliced onion and 6 mint leaves, boil until soft.

Fry lightly in 56 g (2 ozs) of ghee or other fat for 3 or 4 minutes:

    1 onion
    1 clove of garlic } minced.
    2 cloves.
    2 cardamoms.
    A 50 mm (2 inch) stick of cinnamon.

Now add the cooked beans, a generous pinch of black pepper, salt to taste and a squeeze of lemon juice.

Dry Curry of Haricot or Butter Beans

Soak overnight in cold water 225 g ($\frac{1}{2}$ lb) of haricot or butter beans and cook until soft, and then drain.

Fry lightly in oil for 3 or 4 minutes:

1 onion
1 clove of garlic } chopped finely.

Add:

1 teaspoonful of ground turmeric.
$\frac{1}{2}$ teaspoonful of ground cummin seed.
Less than $\frac{1}{2}$ teaspoonful of ground chillies.
Heaped teaspoonful of tomato paste or 2 fresh firm tomatoes, chopped finely.

Continue the gentle cooking for a few minutes longer, then toss the cooked beans lightly in, adding at the same time a dessertspoonful of finely desiccated cocoanut. If too dry add a little of the liquor in which the beans have been boiled, but there really should be no gravy in this curry, and the beans, though well cooked, should not be broken. Salt to taste and a squeeze of lemon juice.

Country Captain of Vegetables

910 g (2 lbs) of cold vegetables, such as potatoes, carrots, turnips, beans, peas, or a mixture of these, are tossed into a basin with a dessertspoonful of curry powder and sprinkled with a dessertspoonful of tamarind water or vinegar, then *sautéd* in a pan in which sliced onions (preferably spring) and garlic have been lightly fried. Salt to taste.

Serve with fresh scraped or desiccated cocoanut sprinkled over it.

Ghota Ka Ghagi

1.4 kg (3 lbs) of spinach, boiled soft and squeezed as dry as possible and thoroughly well pulped.
1 large onion, very finely sliced, or 2 tablespoonfuls of minced spring onions.
2 cloves of garlic, thinly sliced lengthwise.
4 fresh or pickled chillies cut lengthwise.
1 tablespoonful of olive oil or oiled butter.

For about 5 minutes fry lightly in the oil the onions, garlic and chillies. Add the spinach and thoroughly blend it with the other ingredients. Salt to taste.

Any kind of green vegetables can be treated in a like manner

XVII

Foogaths

FOOGATHS are savoury dishes made almost exclusively out of different kinds of vegetables. They are cooked, and that is the essential difference between them and Sambals.

Cocoanut invariably enters into every foogath, and if freshly scraped cocoanut can be obtained it is always preferable to desiccated cocoanut. Oil, either mustard or gingili, is the fat generally used.

Foogaths under various names are eaten by all castes and classes of people throughout India, as there is nothing in them to militate against their common use by either vegetarians or non-vegetarians. Hindus or Mohammedans. Foogaths are endless, for practically every kind of vegetable, green fruit, etc., that is eatable by man can be converted into them.

In almost every English household vegetables are left over, and so often thrown away. A simple foogath is easily made out of these; and, what is more, it is appetizing, tasty, nourishing and can be eaten either by itself or with any other dish.

Drumstick Foogath (*Mooroongkai*)

The drumsticks, having been well washed and scraped and cut into convenient sizes, are boiled in water with a little salt until done and then drained.

Fry lightly in sufficient ghee or other fat for 3 or 4 minutes:

1 onion and 2 or 3 cloves of garlic, sliced finely.

1 teaspoonful of ground turmeric.

1 saltspoonful of ground cummin seed.

½ teaspoonful or less of ground chillies.

Now stir into it 2 dessertspoonfuls of finely desiccated cocoanut or freshly scraped cocoanut, and lastly add the boiled drumsticks. Salt to taste. Stir lightly, as the drumsticks must not be broken.

N.B. – Drumstick leaves and drumstick flowers are also made into foogaths more or less in the same way as Cabbage Foogath.

A Foogath of Beans (*Mochokotay Foogath*)

225 g ($\frac{1}{2}$ lb) of haricot, butter or broad beans can be used, cooked in the ordinary way and drained well.

In a stewpan in sufficient fat fry lightly for 3 or 4 minutes:

1 onion and 2 cloves of garlic, sliced finely.
$\frac{1}{2}$ dozen thin slices of fresh or pickled green ginger.
2 or 3 fresh or pickled chillies, minced finely.

When the onions are sufficiently cooked, but not browned, add the beans and 2 dessertspoonfuls of desiccated cocoanut. Salt to taste.

Banana Foogath (*Kayla ka Foogath*)

6 raw or green bananas, cut in 25 mm (1 inch) lengths and soaked in cold salt and water for an hour or more and then drained.

In 28 g (1 oz) of ghee or other fat fry lightly for 3 or 4 minutes:

1 onion and 2 cloves of garlic, sliced finely.
2 or 3 fresh or pickled chillies, cut lengthwise, in halves.
$\frac{1}{2}$ teaspoonful of fresh or pickled green ginger, finely minced.

Then add:

1 teaspoonful of ground turmeric.
$\frac{1}{2}$ teaspoonful of ground cummin seed.
$\frac{1}{2}$ teaspoonful or less of ground chillies.

Cook on a slow fire for 3 or 4 minutes longer. Now add the bananas. Mix, cover the pan and on a very gentle heat cook until the bananas are soft but not pulped. Now stir into it half of a fresh cocoanut scraped, or 2 dessertspoonfuls of finely desiccated cocoanut. Salt to taste.

Toss lightly and simmer for a few minutes longer with the pan uncovered.

Behndi or Lady's Fingers Foogath

Use the canned Behndis and drain thoroughly.

1 onion
2 cloves of garlic } sliced finely.
6 thin slices of fresh or pickled green ginger
2 or 3 fresh or pickled chillies } minced finely.
$\frac{1}{2}$ teaspoonful of ground chillies.

Fry lightly in 56 g (2 ozs) of ghee or other fat for 3 or 4 minutes all the above ingredients except the Behndis. Then add 2 table-spoonfuls of finely scraped fresh cocoanut or 1 dessertspoonful of desiccated cocoanut. Add the Behndis and salt to taste and simmer gently until they are warmed through.

The addition of 2 or 3 finely sliced tomatoes cooked with the other ingredients before the Behndis are added is an improvement.

Tomato Foogath (*Thucahley Foogath*)

225 g (½ lb) of tomatoes, skinned and chopped.
Fry lightly in ghee or other fat for 3 or 4 minutes:

1 onion	all
2 cloves of garlic	very
½ teaspoonful of fresh or pickled green ginger	finely
3 or 4 fresh or pickled chillies	sliced.

Add the tomatoes and a dessertspoonful of freshly scraped or desiccated cocoanut. Salt to taste and simmer gently with the pan uncovered until there is little or no liquor.

Cabbage Foogath (*Gobee ka Foogath*)

Fry lightly in 56 g (2 ozs) of ghee, oil or other fat:

1 large onion ⎫
2 cloves of garlic ⎬ finely sliced.
4 red or green fresh or pickled chillies or 3 dry red chillies, cut lengthwise and the inner seeds removed.
6 thin slices of green or pickled ginger.

Add to this a medium-sized parboiled cabbage which has been well drained and roughly chopped, together with a little salt. Gradually complete the cooking of the cabbage and add to it a tablespoonful of finely desiccated or grated fresh cocoanut.

Carrot Foogath (*Gager ka Foogath*)

Use raw carrots, roughly grated, parboiled and thoroughly drained in the same way as Cabbage Foogath.

Mooroongakai Foogath

225 g (½ lb) of drumstick leaves broiled slightly and then covered with water and boiled until done and drained thoroughly.

In 56 g (2 ozs) of ghee or oil fry lightly for 3 or 4 minutes:

1 large onion
2 cloves of garlic ⎵ all chopped finely.
4 to 6 fresh or pickled chillies

Add the leaves and half of a freshly-scraped cocoanut, to 2 heaped tablespoonfuls of finely desiccated cocoanut. Salt or taste. Mix thoroughly, continue the frying until you get the foogath fairly dry.

Boorthas

These are Moslem savoury dishes served with Pillaus, Kitcherees and cocoanut rice. They are sometimes eaten with Chuppaties or other Rotis.

Though savoury in character they are not curries in any sense of the word.

Prawn Boortha (Ginga Boortha)

Fry lightly for about 5 minutes in 56 g (2 ozs) of ghee or butter:

1 large onion
1 clove of garlic ⎵ all minced very finely.
1 teaspoonful of green or pickled ginger
¼ teaspoonful of ground chillies.
¼ teaspoonful of ground cummin seed.

Then add either bottled, canned or fresh prawns (which have been previously cooked and shelled), 2 tablespoonfuls of thick cocoanut milk and salt to taste. Warm thoroughly and *serve hot*.

Vegetable Marrow Boortha

Into a saucepan put:

56 g (2 ozs) of ghee or butter.
1 onion
A small clove of garlic ⎵ very finely minced.
A teaspoonful of green or pickled ginger
½ teaspoonful of ground cummin seed.
3 red, green or pickled chillies, chopped coarsely.

Lightly fry all these together for about 5 minutes, but do not brown the onion. Add sufficient marrow which has been previously cut into pieces about 50 mm (2 inches) square and partially cooked. Continue the cooking until the marrow is tender, then mash thoroughly. Add a tablespoonful of finely desiccated or finely grated cocoanut, salt to taste and a squeeze of lemon juice.

Pumpkin Boortha

Made exactly as the Vegetable Marrow Boortha is made.

Tomato Boortha

Scald the tomatoes, remove the skin and beat them up with:

A very finely minced onion.
3 red, green or pickled chillies, chopped coarsely.
1 tablespoonful of finely desiccated or finely grated fresh cocoanut.
½ teaspoonful of olive, mustard or gingili oil.
Salt to taste.

Cucumber Boortha

Peel and cook the cucumber until soft, then drain it thoroughly and mash it with:

1 medium-sized onion
½ clove of garlic   } minced very
½ teaspoonful of green or pickled ginger   finely.
3 green or red fresh or pickled chillies, chopped coarsely.
A tablespoonful of olive, mustard or gingili oil.
Salt to taste.
A squeeze of lemon juice.

Brinjal Boortha

Boil or bake the brinjals, skin and then pulp them with very finely minced onion, chopped green or red chillies, a little very thick cocoanut milk or a tablespoonful of finely grated or desiccated cocoanut, and less than ½ teaspoonful of mustard, gingili or olive oil and salt and lemon juice to taste.

Behndi Boortha

Well boiled Behndi, thoroughly mashed with:

Finely chopped onions.
1 or 2 red or green fresh or pickled chillies.
1 tablespoonful of very thick cocoanut milk or about a
heaped tablespoonful of very finely cut desiccated cocoanut.
Salt and lemon juice to taste.

A little olive, mustard or gingili oil is often added to it.

XVIII

Sambals

MAY be compared to Western hors d'oeuvres, but they are always served as an accompaniment to a main or principal dish. The varieties are almost endless in number depending on the materials available and the skill or taste of the cook.

The recipe for a Sambal dressing and a Sambal sauce can be generally utilized.

Sambal Dressing

In a little ghee or oil fry lightly on a slow fire until the onions are cooked but not browned:

1 large onion
1 clove of garlic } finely minced.
2 green chillies
½ teaspoonful of ground ginger.
¼ teaspoonful of ground cummin seed.
1 teaspoonful of ground turmeric.
1 pinch of ground red chillies.

Sambal Sauce

A cream sauce made with cocoanut milk instead of cow's milk to which are added finely chopped onions, a suspicion of garlic and a fairly generous pinch of ground red chillies.

Salt and lemon juice to taste is used for Sambals made of finely shredded lettuce, tender cabbage or other greens, sliced cucumber, celery, chicory, etc.

Brinjal Sambal (Kutherakai Sambal)

Either boil or roast in the oven a large brinjal until sufficiently cooked, skin it and mash the pulp. Add to the pulp:

1 dessertspoonful of very finely chopped onion.
1 or 2 green chillies also very finely chopped.
1 or 2 tablespoonfuls of thick cocoanut milk.
Salt to taste.

Prawn Sambals (*Ginga Ka Sambal – Yerrah Sambal*)

Chopped cooked prawns blended with a sufficiency of Sambal dressing with a dessertspoonful of thick cocoanut milk and a heaped dessertspoonful of finely desiccated cocoanut. Salt and lemon juice to taste.

These Sambals can be served either hot or cold and are usually garnished with slices of hard-boiled eggs.

Lobster or Crab Sambal (*Anglo-Indian*)

Blend lobster or crab meat with a sufficiency of Sambal dressing or sauce.

Lobster or crab meat chopped, is treated in the same way as fish or prawn sambals, but it is advisable to use thick cocoanut milk as well as a little fresh scraped cocoanut. Salt and lemon juice to taste.

Served either hot or cold.

Tomato Sambal (*Belatee Bygun Ka Sambal*)

This is a blend of finely sliced fresh tomatoes and onions, 1 or 2 green chillies chopped finely, lemon juice, pepper and salt to taste, and when dished sprinkled over with desiccated or freshly grated cocoanut.

Potato Sambal (*Aloo ka Sambal*)

Cooked potato cut in cubes the size of dice, lightly blended with chopped green chillies and a pinch of ground red chillies, $\frac{1}{2}$ teaspoonful of very finely chopped onions or preferably spring onions sliced and with a little of the green, a sprinkling of olive oil. Salt and lemon juice to taste.

Potato Sambal (*Aloo ka Sambal*)

(Another way)

Cold mashed potato, blended with finely chopped onions, preferably spring onions, ground red chillies, and salt and lemon juice to taste.

If too dry add a little cream, milk or cocoanut milk.

Cold Potato Sambal (*Aloo ka Sambal*)

Mash the potatoes thoroughly well with:

A very finely minced onion.
3 red or green, fresh or pickled chillies, chopped coarsely.
A tablespoonful of very thick cocoanut milk and a table-
    spoonful of finely desiccated cocoanut or fresh grated
    cocoanut.
$\frac{1}{2}$ teaspoonful of olive, mustard or gingili oil.
Juice of $\frac{1}{2}$ a lemon and salt to taste.

Potato Sambal (*Aloo ka Sambal*)

(Another way)

Mashed potato mixed with a Sambal dressing, but with the
addition of finely desiccated cocoanut and a very little thick
cocoanut milk. Salt and lemon juice to taste. Serve either hot or
cold.

Sambal of Mixed Vegetables (*Tharkari ka Sambal*)

Use a macedoine containing carrots, peas, beans, turnips and
potatoes and treat exactly in the same way as Tomato Sambal.

Egg Sambal (*Undah ka Sambal*)

Hard-boiled eggs cut lengthwise in quarters are lightly blended
with very finely chopped onions, fresh green or pickled chillies,
oil, lemon juice and salt to taste, and when dished up, sprinkled
over with finely desiccated or fresh scraped cocoanut.

Prawn and Egg Sambal (*Ginga aur Undah ka Sambal*)

Whole prawns and hard-boiled eggs cut in halves and smothered
with a cream sauce in which thick cocoanut milk has been
blended and flavoured with a little finely chopped onion, 2 fresh
green or red chillies cut in fine strips. Salt and lemon juice to
taste, and garnished with green peas.

This dish can be utilized as a cold luncheon dish.

Fish Sambals (*Muchlee ka Sambal*)

Blend flaked, cooked fish of any kind with a sufficiency of Sambal mixture made as above and add a dessertspoonful of finely desiccated cocoanut and a teaspoonful of chopped parsley. Salt and lemon juice to taste. Serve either hot or cold.

Cold Chicken Sambal (*Moorgee ka Sambal*)

A shredded chicken breast tossed in freshly scraped cocoanut and dusted over with ground red chillies. Salt and lemon juice to taste, or blended with the Sambal sauce.

Butter or Haricot Beans Sambal (*Mochokotay Sambal*)

Cooked butter or haricot beans sprinkled over with ground red chillies, or fresh or pickled chillies, or salt and lemon juice to taste or tossed in the Sambal mixture.

Lady's Fingers Sambal (*Behndi Sambal*)

Canned lady's fingers flavoured with finely chopped onions, red or green chillies, salt and lemon juice to taste, and sprinkled over with finely desiccated cocoanut.

Onion Sambal (*Peaz ka Sambal*)

Very finely sliced onion, fresh or pickled chillies cut lengthwise, a pinch of ground red chillies and salt and lemon juice to taste.

Banana Sambals (*Kayla ka Sambal*)

Firm green bananas cut into fairly thin slices sprinkled over with ground red chillies or finely chopped fresh or pickled chillies. Salt and lemon juice to taste, or blended with the Sambal sauce.

Cocoanut Sambal (*Thainga Sambal*)

Finely desiccated cocoanut well blended with finely chopped onions, ground red chillies and salt and lemon juice to taste.

Apple Sambal (Sa-oo ka Sambal)

Sour apples cut into small dice and sprinkled over with ground red chillies, salt and lemon juice to taste, or blended with the Sambal sauce.

Fresh Chutneys

THESE are prepared freshly and in quantities sufficient for the
day. They are usually eaten with curry and rice, sometimes only
with rice. Their consistency should be that of potted meat.

These chutneys are always made hot with chillies, but are
taken sparingly, even as mustard with meat. There is no reason,
however, why they should not be made milder and more acceptable to Western palates.

In India they are ground on a curry stone, but they can be
produced with an ordinary pestle and mortar, preferably marble.

Mint Chutney (Poothena Chutney)

On a curry stone or in a mortar reduce a heaped teaspoonful
of tamarind (freed from stones and fibres) to a fine paste and
gradually pound into it a handful or more of fresh mint leaves,
4 to 6 dry red chillies or fresh or pickled chillies and 2 cloves of
garlic. Salt to taste.

This chutney should be of the consistency of potted meat.
If necessary moisten with a few drops of vinegar.

Cocoanut Chutney (Thainga Chutney)

½ of a finely scraped cocoanut or 2 heaped tablespoonfuls
   of desiccated cocoanut.
6 slices of fresh or pickled green ginger.
3 or 4 dry red or fresh or pickled chillies.
A clove or two of garlic.
Salt to taste.

The above ingredients are blended and pounded together into a
paste with the addition of a little lemon juice.

Sometimes, the cocoanut used in making the chutney, instead
of being scraped, is slightly roasted on a Thoa or griddle and then
pounded.

Tamarind Chutney (*Pullee or Imli Chutney*)

Free the required amount of tamarind from fibres and seeds and pound it into a paste in a mortar with a little garlic, chillies, either fresh or dry, and a very little green ginger. Salt to taste.

Dhall Chutney (*Purpoo Chutney*)

Broil slightly 113 g ($\frac{1}{4}$ lb) of Toor Dhall (Egyptian lentils will do) and pound it into a paste, moistening it occasionally with lemon juice and blending the following into it:

  2 cloves of garlic.
  4 to 6 chillies.
  6 thin slices of fresh or pickled green ginger.
  Salt to taste.

Coriander Chutney (*Kothmir Chutney*)

A large handful of picked green coriander leaves is pounded into a paste with green chillies, green ginger and garlic. Salt and lemon juice to taste.

Green coriander is easily grown in shallow boxes like mustard and cress, either under glass or in the open in the summer time. Chilli plants grown under glass will bear fruit, but the chillies will not be as pungent as in the East.

Green Tomato Chutney (*Thucahley Chutney*)

This is made in exactly the same way as coriander chutney, but blended in with it is a piece of fresh cocoanut or a proportion of desiccated cocoanut.

Mooroongakai Chutney

Remove the inside of boiled Drumstick and grind it with green chillies, garlic, tamarind, green ginger, onions and salt to taste.

XX

Bhugias

113 g (¼ lb) of flour.
1 teaspoonful of ground turmeric.
¼ teaspoonful of ground chillies.
2 heaped teaspoonfuls of finely minced onions (spring onions
    preferred).
½ teaspoonful of garlic, finely minced.
2 fresh or pickled chillies, chopped finely.
4 tablespoonfuls of cooked vegetable, preferably a mixture
    of peas, carrots and turnips, or any of them.
2 eggs.
Milk.
Salt.

Mix the flour, turmeric, ground chillies, onions, garlic and
chopped chillies together, and mix into a thick batter with the
eggs and if necessary a little milk. Then add the vegetables,
drained, with salt to taste and stir lightly so that the vegetables
are not pulped.

Cook by dropping a dessertspoonful of the mixture into deep
boiling fat.

The Bhugias will swell out like doughnuts and when a golden
brown, drain and serve.

Prawn Bhugias

113 g (¼ lb) of cooked prawns cut up in pieces.
113 g (¼ lb) of flour.
½ teaspoonful of ground turmeric.
A pinch of ground chillies.
2 fresh or pickled chillies.
1 small onion ⎫
1 clove of garlic ⎬ chopped finely.
4 mint leaves ⎭
2 eggs slightly beaten.
Salt.

Mix the flour, turmeric and ground chillies together. Then add the finely chopped onions, garlic, chillies and mint, and with the 2 eggs convert this dry mixture into a thick batter. If the batter is too stiff add a little milk, fresh or sour.

Now mix in the prawns, salt to taste and cook by dropping a dessertspoonful of the mixture into deep boiling fat. Cook until the Bhugias are a golden colour. Drain.

Rice Bhugias

225 g ($\frac{1}{2}$ lb) of rice flour.
1 teaspoonful of ground turmeric.
$\frac{1}{2}$ teaspoonful of ground cummin seed.
$\frac{1}{2}$ teaspoonful of ground red chillies or 2 or 3 fresh red or green chillies very finely chopped.
1 onion and a small clove of garlic also very finely minced.
2 eggs.
Salt to taste.
Lard or oil for frying.

Mix all the dry ingredients together and convert it into a thick batter with the eggs. If necessary add a little water. Drop a spoonful of this mixture into deep boiling fat until a golden colour. Drain and serve hot.

Soojee Bhugia

225 g ($\frac{1}{2}$ lb) of fine Soojee.
2 eggs.
1 heaped tablespoonful of onions (chopped finely).
2 cloves of garlic (chopped finely).
Chopped red or green chillies (fresh or pickled) to taste.
$\frac{1}{2}$ teaspoonful of very finely chopped green or pickled ginger.
Salt.

Beat up the eggs in a basin and mix into it the onion, garlic, chillies and ginger. Work in the soojee flour, and if necessary add sufficient milk to make the mixture into a thick batter. Salt to taste.

Drop spoonfuls of the batter into boiling fat. Fry slowly until the fritters are a golden colour. Drain and serve hot.

Philouries (Dhall Fritters)

Chenna flour (Basun) is usually used, but any other Dhall flour can be used for this.

Mix together:

> 225 g (½ lb) of Dhall flour.
> ½ teaspoonful of ground turmeric.
> ½ teaspoonful of ground cummin seed.
> ½ teaspoonful of ground red chillies.
> 2 red or green, fresh or pickled chillies   } minced
> 2 cloves of garlic   finely.
> 1 large onion.

Mix together these ingredients into a thick batter with a beaten egg, salt to taste and a sufficiency of sour milk or curds.

Drop spoonfuls of the batter into deep boiling fat and cook to a golden brown.

Philouries (Soojee Fritters)

Mix together:

> 225 g (½ lb) of Soojee.
> ½ teaspoonful of ground turmeric.
> ½ teaspoonful of ground cummin seed.
> ½ teaspoonful of ground red chillies.

Then add to it:

> 1 or 2 cloves of garlic   }
> 12 spring onions with their green stalks   minced
> 6 thin slices of fresh or pickled green   finely.
>   ginger

Convert this into a thick batter with the addition of sour milk, an egg and a pinch of salt.

Drop spoonfuls of the batter into deep boiling fat and fry until a golden brown.

Dhall Kara Pooree (Hot Savoury Dhall Pastry)

Moong Dhall is generally used, but Egyptian lentils will answer.

225 g (½ lb) of lentils well washed and boiled in only enough water to be absorbed by the lentils. Pulp thoroughly, add:

113 g (¼ lb) of pastry whites.
1 teaspoonful of ground turmeric.
½ teaspoonful of ground red chillies.
½ teaspoonful of finely minced green or pickled ginger.
A tablespoonful of chopped spring onions.
A clove of garlic finely minced.
2 or 3 fresh or pickled green or red chillies.
A generous pinch of ground cummin seed.
1 egg and salt to taste.

Mix thoroughly and drop spoonfuls of it into boiling fat and fry until a golden colour. This pooree is made to differ in flavour by using different kinds of Dhall.

Kara Vuddays

Madras is famous for its Vuddays which are seldom made at home. They are made in the Bazaars and hawked round the town just as Muffins and Crumpets were in England. The makers are usually Hindus who make various savoury biscuits or Poorees.

Kara Vuddays are made as follows:

Ooduth – known as Ooloonthoo in Madras – is well washed and set to soak in cold water for 24 hours, then thoroughly drained, and either pounded in a wooden mortar or ground on a curry stone into a coarse flour. This is blended with ground turmeric, chillies, cummin seed, chopped green chillies, spring onions and garlic, salted to taste and converted into a stiff dough with water. A piece of this, the size of a golf ball, is placed on a well-damped cloth and another damped cloth is spread over it. The ball of dough is then pressed down to form a flat round cake about 12 mm (½ inch) in thickness. With the forefinger the upper cloth is pressed right through the centre of the Vudday. The cloth is then removed and the Vudday will be found in shape like an ordinary almond ring.

To Cook. – Drop the Vuddays one by one into deep boiling fat – preferably oil – and when cooked, drain.

XXI

Pustholes and Samoosas

THESE are puffs made of the very finest wheat flour (Mydah) with ghee or butter. They are made in different sizes: semicircular in shape in the Deccan and Southern India; triangular and circular in Bombay, Bengal and the North generally. The fillings are of different kinds – savoury or sweet, vegetarian and non-vegetarian.

Pustholes and Samoosas are carried on long journeys in India and the East as sandwiches are in Western countries.

Pastry for Pustholes and Samoosas

The pastry is made by lightly rubbing into 450 g (1 lb) of the very finest white flour (Mydah) 113 g (4 ozs) of ghee or butter and $\frac{1}{2}$ a teaspoonful of salt and converting it into a paste with the addition of milk or milk and water (preferably sour milk).

Knead until the pastry feels soft and velvety to the touch and is extremely pliable, then roll it out to the thickness of a penny, stamp out circular pieces 50 mm (2 inches) in diameter and in the centre of each piece place a spoonful of the mince curry or other filling. Wet the edge of the pastry and turn one half over the other half, press down and fry in ghee or other fat to a golden colour. Drain on kitchen paper.

The pastry for Samoosas is made in exactly the same way as for Curry Pustholes. The fillings, however, are more in the nature of freshly prepared chutneys, such as Poothena (mint), Copra (cocoanut), Imli (tarmarind), etc.

Mince Curry for Pustholes

225 g ($\frac{1}{2}$ lb) of finely minced lean mutton or beef.
56 g (2 ozs) of ghee or other fat.
1 dozen spring onions (part of the green stems as well).
1 clove of garlic.
A 12 mm ($\frac{1}{2}$ inch) piece of fresh or pickled green ginger.
2 whole cloves.

2 whole cardamoms.
A 50 mm (2 inch) stick of cinnamon.
1 dessertspoonful of curry powder or curry paste.
Salt and lemon juice.

In the ghee or other fat fry lightly for 3 or 4 minutes the chopped ingredients and spices, then add the curry powder or paste. Mix and continue the cooking for another 2 or 3 minutes.

Add the meat, mix thoroughly, cover the pan and simmer the contents until the meat is cooked. Add salt and lemon juice to taste. Watch the cooking of this curry, for it cooks in its own juice and is likely to get too dry. If necessary, add a little water now and again to help the cooking of the meat, but not enough to pulp it.

Curry puffs are said to ward off sea-sickness. The other principal fillings are:

Dhall curry, made in the Mogul style.
Meeta Dhall, made in the Mogul style.
Dry vegetable curries (various).
Foogaths, etc.

XXII

Chuppatis, Parattas, Rotis Appums

THE breads of India vary in different parts. Some are leavened, others unleavened, different kinds of meal or flour being used in the making. Wheat bulks largely in the food of the people, so much so that it stands next to rice in importance as a food crop.

Wheat flour is, as in Western countries, of different grades. The principal grades in India are known as:

(1) Soojee or Rolong, which is akin to wheat semolina.
(2) Atta – a wholemeal flour.
(3) Myday – equivalent or even superior in fineness to the best pastry whites.

The wheat chupatties and other rotis made of Jowari, Chenna flour (Basun), etc., are eaten every day by many millions of both Hindus and Mohammedans. In Southern India, rice being much more consumed than in the North, wheat flour is not used so largely; but rice flour, Raggie flour, Cholum and Cumboo are extensively utilized for making their breads, and in the South leaven in the shape of Toddy is frequently used.

The following recipes are produced to show how easily and with what simple utensils and fuelling they can be made.

With Western conveniences there is practically no trouble in producing these breads (except Hoppers), which in so many hundreds of cases have been the food for many years of English men and women in India. Dhall Roti, Kabab Roti must be familiar to many.

Instructions for Baking Chupatties, etc.

A thoa, or griddle, wiped over with a greased cloth is heated on a slow fire. The Chupattie is then placed on it and turned over now and again until it is cooked and slightly browned, but not hardened. The griddle will need wiping over with a greased cloth every time a Chupattie is baked.

Chupatties (Unleavened Wheaten Cakes)

Atta is coarse Indian flour, but equal quantities of ordinary white flour and wholemeal flour mixed and sifted together will give exactly the same results.

Take 225 g ($\frac{1}{2}$ lb) of this mixture, add a generous pinch of salt and rub into it an ounce of ghee or butter. Convert into a soft dough with cold water, cover and stand aside for an hour or longer. Then knead well, divide into balls the size of a billiard ball and roll each out to the size of a teaplate. Bake on a thoa or griddle.

In India the balls of dough are clapped out between the palms of the hands into flat cakes.

Sweet Chupatties

225 g ($\frac{1}{2}$ lb) of wholemeal flour
225 g ($\frac{1}{2}$ lb) of white flour $\Big\}$ sieved together.

Then lightly rub into it 113 g ($\frac{1}{4}$ lb) of ghee or butter and convert it into a dough with about 6 tablespoonfuls of dark brown soft sugar dissolved in a very little water. Knead the dough and form into flat cakes about twice the thickness of a penny and about the size of a teaplate.

Bake on both sides on a thoa (griddle) which has been greased.

Rice Flour Chupatties

Rice flour with salt to taste is made into a dough with boiling water, covered and set aside for an hour. Then kneaded thoroughly and formed it balls about the size of a billiard ball. These balls are rolled or clapped out to the size of a teaplate and then baked on a thoa or griddle. See Baking Instructions (page 128).

To Prepare Rice Flour

Rice flour is sold by all the large stores. In India, however, it is usually prepared at home in the following manner:

The rice is thoroughly well washed and dried – usually spread on a mat in the sun – then either ground in a stone mill (Chukkee) or pounded in a wooden mortar with a wooden pestle and sifted through fine muslin until the flour feels silky to the touch.

Jowari Roti or Chupatties

This is made in exactly the same way as Rice Flour Chupatties. Jowari flour is used, and the cakes are similar but thicker. As Jowari flour is not easily obtainable outside India, barley meal or fine oatmeal will answer the purpose.

Parattas (Deccan Wheaten Cakes)

The very finest flour, called Mydah, is used, but ordinary pastry whites will answer the purpose.

Into 225 (½ lb) of the finest flour obtainable rub in lightly 56 g (2 ozs) of ghee or butter with a pinch of salt. Convert into a soft dough and knead well until it feels velvety and is absolutely pliable. Using your hands, roll it out into a long roll about 25 mm (1 inch) in diameter. Cut this roll into inch lengths and flatten them down end on with your fingers. On each piece put a spot of ghee or butter and place them one on top of the other so that there is ghee or butter between each two pieces, using 4 to 6 pieces for each cake. Flatten these out and roll them with a rolling pin into cakes about the size of a large teaplate. These cakes must be fried on a slow fire in a frying-pan containing a little ghee or oil. Butter will not do, as the Parattas are very liable to burn if butter is used. Cook on both sides, using more ghee if necessary, as ghee gets absorbed in the cooking, but do not brown or harden. When properly handled and cooked the Parattas will be flaky.

Phoolkay

Lightly rub 28 to 56 g (1 to 2 ozs) of ghee or butter into 225 g (½ lb) of Mydah or best pastry whites, with a generous pinch of salt in it. Convert into a soft dough, knead well and put aside for an hour. Then knead again thoroughly and form into balls the size of a billiard ball. Roll each out into very thin flat cakes and bake on a thoa or griddle as Chupatties are baked. The lightness of Phoolkay depends on the kneading.

Atta Roti

225 g (½ lb) of Atta (equal parts of wholemeal and white flour) and a pinch of salt is mixed into a soft dough with a well-beaten egg and a little sour milk, thoroughly kneaded and made into

six round flat, thin biscuits about the size of a small teaplate. These are baked on a thoa, or griddle, on both sides.

Rice and Cocoanut Bread

450 g (1 lb) of rice flour.
113 g ($\frac{1}{4}$ lb) of freshly scraped or finely desiccated cocoanut.
113 g ($\frac{1}{4}$ lb) of soft sugar.

Mix together and make into a stiff dough with a little boiling water. Portions of the dough are then flattened out into round biscuits about 75 or 100 mm (3 or 4 inches) in diameter and 6 mm ($\frac{1}{4}$ inch) in thickness.

Bake first on one side and then on the other on a greased thoa (griddle).

Madras Hoppers (*Appum*)

A batter is made overnight with about 450 g (1 lb) of the very finest rice flour, a pinch of salt, a gill of toddy and thin cocoanut milk. In the morning sufficient thick cocoanut milk is well whipped into it to make a batter the consistency of pancake mixture.

Hoppers are cooked in what are known as "hopper chatties" – shallow earthenware pans. The fuel is generally charcoal. One chatty is put on a slow charcoal or wood fire and the bottom of the inside is wiped over with a ghee-greased cloth. A ladleful of the batter is then poured into the chatty, where it spreads out into a flat cake. Another chatty (similar in size) filled with live charcoal is placed on top of the chatty in which the hopper is, and a damp cloth is placed right round where the upper chatty rests on the lower one. This is done to keep the steam in.

In a very few minutes the hopper is baked and easily removed. It is thick in the centre (owing to the shallow shape of the chatty), pitted like a crumpet and whitish in colour. The rim is thin and light brown. When the hopper is taken out of the pan it is brushed over with thick cocoanut milk with a feather and covered over with a cloth to keep warm. The chatty is greased between every two bakings.

Brown Hoppers (also known as Black Hoppers) are made with brown rice flour.

Egg Hoppers have the yolks of eggs, a little sugar, and a few caraway seeds added to the Hopper mixture.

Raggie Roti

Coarse Raggie flour is made into a dough with boiling milk or water in which coarse brown sugar has been dissolved. The dough is well kneaded, divided into balls which are pressed into flat cakes between the palms of the hansd, and baked on both sides on a thoa or griddle.

Soup—Mulligatawny—Shoorva—Russam

MULLIGATAWNY soup as made for Europeans and Anglo-Indians resident in India is anglicized to a very large extent. In Southern India the term Mulligatunny, which literally means pepper or chilli water, indicates the character of this dish, and whenever a dry curry is eaten, pepper water of some kind or other is served with it.

To Prepare Tamarind Water for Mulligatawny, Pepper Water, etc.

56 g (2 ozs) of ripe tamarinds are well macerated in 570 ml (1 pint) of cold water, freed from seeds and fibres and then strained through a fairly coarse sieve or Tammy.

Mulligatawny – Mulligatunny

(Made with ordinary Meat Stock and using MulligatawnyPaste) In a dessertspoonful of ghee or other fat, fry lightly 1 onion and 1 clove of garlic, finely minced. Add 1 heaped dessertspoonful of mulligatawny paste and 1 dessertspoonful of tomato paste or tomato purée. Fry for 2 or 3 minutes, then turn into it a quart of stock. Bring to the boil. Salt and lemon jucie to taste. If desired, thicken with a little flour and strain.

Consommé Mulligatawny (Anglo-Indian)

2.3 l (2 quarts) of good chicken stock
1 onion chopped up
2 cloves
2 heaped tablespoonfuls of pepper
   water mixture

tied loosely in a muslin bag.

Bring the stock to boiling point, then add all the other ingredients tied in a muslin bag. Lower the gas and simmer gently for half an hour. Clear in the usual way. Add salt to taste and serve with boiled rice.

Mulligatawny – Mulligatunny

(With ordinary Meat Stock)

1.1 l (1 quart) of stock.
285 ml ($\frac{1}{2}$ pint) of thick cocoanut milk.
1 small onion and a clove of garlic, finely chopped.
3 or 4 thin slices of fresh or pickled green ginger.
28 g (1 oz) of ghee or butter.
1 level dessertspoonful of ground corianders.
$\frac{1}{2}$ a small teaspoonful of ground turmeric.
$\frac{1}{2}$ a small teaspoonful of ground chillies.
$\frac{1}{2}$ a small teaspoonful of ground fenugreek.
$\frac{1}{2}$ a small teaspoonful of ground cummin seed.
Salt ot taste.

Fry on a slow fire in the ghee or butter, the onions, garlic and
green ginger, then add the other ground ingredients. Stir and cook
for a minute or two. Add the stock, allow it to come gradually
to the boil, then add the cocoanut milk and salt to taste. Simmer
gently for 5 to 10 minutes, then serve. The pan must be uncovered
the whole time and the soup is not usually strained.

Serve with boiled rice.

Chicken Mulligatawny (*Moorgee Shoorva*)

A chicken cut up into 12 or more pieces. Cover with about
2.3 l (2 quarts) of cold water, add a few peppercorns. Bring to the
boil, then simmer gently until the chicken is tender.

Mix into a paste with a *very little* vinegar:

1 teaspoonful of ground turmeric.
$\frac{1}{2}$ teaspoonful of ground ginger or 6 thin slices of fresh
　　green or pickled ginger.
1 dessertspoonful of ground corianders.

In another pan, put in a dessertspoonful of ghee or other fat,
1 or 2 dry chillies with the inner seeds removed and a finely
sliced onion. Cook, but do not brown the onions. Now add
the paste, mix and continue the slow cooking for 4 or 5 minutes.
Then turn the contents of the first pan into the second. Let it
boil up. Salt to taste.

Chicken Mulligatawny (*Khoiee Mulligatunny*)

(Made with Mulligatawny Paste)
(Another way)

A chicken cut up into convenient pieces, covered with sufficient water, brought to the boil and simmered until the meat is tender.

In another pan, fry lightly, but do not brown, in a dessertspoonful of ghee or other fat, a small onion and 1 clove of garlic, finely minced, and mix into it 1 heaped dessertspoonful of mulligatawny paste. Stir throughly. Cook for 3 or 4 minutes, and then add the contents of the first pan to the second. Let it boil up and simmer gently for 10 minutes. Salt to taste.

Chicken Curry Soup (*Anglo-Indian*)

1 chicken cut up into convenient pieces.
2 tablespoonfuls of finely chopped onion.
2 cloves of garlic, finely chopped.
½ teaspoonful of ground turmeric.
6 thin slices of green or pickled ginger.
A generous pinch of ground chillies.
56 g (2 ozs) of ghee or butter.

Fry for 4 or 5 minutes in the ghee or butter the onions, garlic, turmeric, ginger, ground chillies and the chicken. Then pour over it about 2.3 l (2 quarts) of stock or water. Bring to the boil, then simmer on a slow fire with the lid of the pan on until the chicken is tender. Salt and lemon juice to taste.

Mutton Mulligatawny (*Gosht ka Shoorva*)

Add to a 1.1 l (1 quart) of mutton stock:

1 onion, very finely sliced.
2 dry chillies, cut lengthwise, and the inner seeds removed.
6 peppercorns.

Bring to the boil, simmer gently until the onions are cooked.

Using another pan, fry for a minute or two on a slow fire in 1 dessertspoonful or less of ghee or other fat:

1 clove of garlic, very finely minced.
1 teaspoonful of ground turmeric.

Now strain the contents of the first pan into the second. Add a little of the lean mutton (used in making the stock) shredded finely, and 2 tablespoonfuls of thick cocoanut milk. Salt and lemon juice to taste. Bring to the boil and then simmer gently for 10 minutes before serving.

Mulligatawny (Mulligatunny)

(Made with Vegetable Stock and Mulligatawny Paste)

This is made exactly in the same way as when meat stock is used. It is customary, however, to add a tablespoonful of thick cocoanut milk just before serving.

Dhall Mulligatawny (Dhall Shoorva)

225 g (¼ lb) of Moosa or other Dhall and 2 tablespoonfuls of chopped onion, boiled soft in 2.3 l (2 quarts) of water and passed through a sieve or tammy.

1 large onion   chopped
A clove of garlic   very
3 or 4 thin slices of fresh or pickled   finely.
   green ginger

2 green or red chillies or 2 dried red chillies, cut lengthwise in halves and the inner seeds removed.

28 g (1 oz) of ghee or butter.

2 tablespoonfuls of Dhye or Tyre (sour curds).

Salt to taste.

Fry the chopped ingredients and chillies in ghee or butter, but do not brown them. Add the Dhall stock, Dhye or sour curds and salt to taste. Stir, bring to the boil and, if preferred, strain again.

Dhall Mulligatawny

(Made with Mulligatawny Paste)
(Another way)

Using 2 pans

1st Pan – Boil in a quart of cold water 113 g (¼ lb) of well-washed Moosa Dhall or Egyptian lentils, 6 peppercorns and 1 onion finely sliced. Cook until the Dhall is soft enough to be passed through a coarse sieve.

2nd Pan – Fry lightly in a dessertspoonful of ghee or other fat, 1 onion and 1 clove of garlic finely sliced. Stir into it a heaped dessertspoonful of mulligatawny paste. Cook for 2 or 3 minutes, and then add the contents of the first pan to the second. Mix well, bring to the boil. Salt to taste.

Dhall Purée (Meeta Dhall Shoorva)

113 g ($\frac{1}{4}$ lb) of Dhall or lentils
1 small onion chopped finely $\Big\}$ boiled to a pulp.

Fry lightly for 2 or 3 minutes in 56 g (2 ozs) of ghee or other fat:
1 onion
1 clove of garlic $\Big\}$ chopped finely.

Add to it:

$\frac{1}{2}$ teaspoonful of ground turmeric.
$\frac{1}{2}$ teaspoonful of chopped fresh or pickled ginger.
1 pinch of ground pepper.
1 pinch of ground chillies.
1 pinch of ground cummin seed.

Continue the frying for a couple of minutes longer. Then add the boiled Dhall to it. Salt and lemon juice to taste.

If the purée is too thick thin it down with a little cocoanut milk or cow's milk.

Rice Soup (Indian)

This is usually the water in which rice has been boiled, flavoured with very finely chopped onions, white pepper, chopped fresh or pickled chillies or ground chillies. Simmer until the onions are cooked. Salt and lemon juice to taste.

If the soup is too thin, thicken with a little ground rice.

Rice Purée (Anglo-Indian)

Boil 225 g ($\frac{1}{2}$ lb) of well-washed Burma rice and 2 tablespoonfuls of chopped onion in 2.3 l (2 quarts) of water until the rice is cooked to a pulp, adding more water if necessary. Rub this through a sieve, and with sufficient milk (or cocoanut milk) bring to the consistency of a purée. Salt and pepper to taste. Now bring the purée again to the boil. Remove from the fire and stir in the yolk of an egg and a tablespoonful or more of shredded fresh Pepperoni (Koffree Chillies).

Plain Pepper Water (*Moloo Tunny*)

This is made with tamarind water, and there is practically no substance in it. It is utilized to moisten the rice when the curry served is perfectly dry. Tamarind water is made by macerating a lump of tamarind about the size of a small tangerine in 1.1 l (2 pints) of warm water and straining.

In a very little ghee or other fat, fry lightly an onion and:

    2 cloves of garlic, thinly sliced.
    1 dessertspoonful of ground corianders.
    1 teaspoonful of ground turmeric.
    1 teaspoonful of ground cummin seed.
    ½ teaspoonful of ground mustard seed.
    6 peppercorns.
    2 or 3 dry red chillies.

Add the strained tamarind water, salt to taste. Boil up and then simmer for 10 or 15 minutes.

Plain Pepper Water (*Moloo Tunny*)

(Another way)

2 Pans are used for this.

    570 ml (1 pint) of tamarind water.
    ½ teaspoonful of ground turmeric.
    ½ teaspoonful of ground mustard seed.
    ½ teaspoonful of ground cummin seed.
    ¼ teaspoonful of ground chillies.
    ¼ teaspoonful of ground fenugreek.
    ½ teaspoonful of whole peppercorns.

Broil the dry ingredients together for a minute or two then add the tamarind water and bring to the boil gradually, and let it simmer for 10 minutes or so. Now get ready the second pan in which you fry, in a tablespoonful of ghee or other fat, a small onion and 2 cloves of garlic, very finely sliced together with 2 dry red chillies. Let the onions cook thoroughly, but do not brown them.

Now, using a fairly coarse strainer, strain the contents of the first pan into the second. Add salt to taste. Bring to the boil and serve.

Dhall Pepper Water (Purpoo Mulligatunny)

56 g (2 ozs) of Moosa Dhall or lentils, boiled till soft in 1.1 l (1 quart) of water.

In 28 g (1 oz) of ghee or other fat, fry lightly for 2 or 3 minutes:
2 tablespoonfuls of chopped onions.
1 clove of garlic, finely sliced.
2 or 3 dry red chillies.
1 dessertspoonful of ground corianders.
1 teaspoonful of ground turmeric.
½ teaspoonful of ground mustard seed.
½ teaspoonful of ground cummin seed.
1 saltspoonful of ground fenugreek.
6 peppercorns.

Then add the boiled Dhall, I teaspoonful of tamarind pulp, and salt to taste.

Bring to the boil and simmer for 10 or 15 minutes. This Dhall is not strained.

Dhall Pepper Water (Purpoo Mulligatunny)

(Another way)

Use 2 pans.
1st Pan:

56 g (2 ozs) of Moosa Dhall or lentils ⎫ boiled in 1.1 l (1 qt.)
1 tablespoonful of chopped onions   ⎬ of water until the
2 dry red chillies   ⎭ lentil is quite soft.

2nd Pan – Fry lightly in an ounce of ghee or other fat, 2 cloves of garlic and an onion finely sliced. Then add to it a heaped tablespoonful of pepper water mixture and continue the frying for a few minutes longer. Now add the contents of the first pan to the second. Salt and tamarind pulp to taste, and a tablespoonful of thick cocoanut milk if desired. Boil up and serve either strained through a coarse strainer or, if preferred, not strained.

Dhall Pepper Water (Purpoo Moloo Tunny)

(Another way)

Using 2 Pans – 113 g (¼ lb) of any kind of Dhall well washed and soaked for an hour or two and then boiled to a pulp in about 1.1 l (1 quart) of water. Mix into it 1 tablespoonful of thick tamarind pulp.

Fry in another pan in sufficient ghee, oil or other fat for a few minutes:

1 tablespoonful of chopped onions.
1 or 2 cloves of garlic, sliced finely.
½ teaspoonful of ground pepper.
½ teaspoonful of ground fenugreek.
1 teaspoonful of ground cummin seed.
1 teaspoonful of ground mustard seed.

When the onions are sufficiently cooked, add the boiling contents of the first pan to the second. Salt to taste, and serve.

Vegetable Pepper Water (Mulligatunny)

(Made with Pepper Water Mixture)

Use 1.1 l (1 quart) of vegetable stock or water in which a piece of tamarind the size of a large walnut has been macerated and then strained.

In a dessertspoonful of ghee or other fat, fry lightly a small onion and a clove of garlic finely sliced. To this is added a heaped tablespoonful of pepper water mixture, then well mixed and cooked on a slow fire for 2 or 3 minutes longer, and then the strained stock and salt to taste are added and brought to the boil before serving.

This soup is very much improved if a tablespoonful of tomato purée is added to the stock or if fresh tomatoes are used in making the stock.

Fish Pepper Water

This is made in exactly the same way as the vegetable pepper water except that the stock is a fish stock made with small pieces of salt fish and to which a dessertspoonful of tamarind pulp has been added.

This stock is not strained, and in addition 2 or 3 red chillies from which the inner seeds have been removed are fried with the onions and garlic before the stock is added.

Meat Pepper Water (Mulligatunny)

Use 1.1 l (1 quart) of meat stock in which a dessertspoonful of tomato pulp has been added, and proceed in the same way as directed for vegetable pepper water.

Pepper Water (*Moloo Tunny*)

Fry light for 2 or 3 minutes in a dessertspoonful of ghee or other fat, 1 small onion and a clove of garlic, very finely minced. Then add a heaped dessertspoonful of pepper water mixture, a teaspoonful of curry powder and a dessertspoonful of tomato paste. Stir well, and fry for 2 or 3 minutes longer.

Now add 1.1 l (1 quart) of good stock (either meat, fish or vegetable) that has been strained. Salt and lemon juice to taste, and *let it boil up*.

This soup must never be thickened. If preferred, it may be strained before serving, but this is not usual.

Chicken Pepper Water (*Khoiee Mulligatunny*)

1st Pan – Cut up a chicken in 12 or more pieces. Cover with about 2.3 l (2 quarts) of cold water, and add to it 2 or 3 dry chillies, cut lengthwise and with inner seeds removed. Then add:

12 peppercorns.
$\frac{1}{2}$ teaspoonful of ground mustard seed.
$\frac{1}{2}$ teaspoonful of ground cummin seed.
2 teaspoonfuls of ground corianders.

Mix thoroughly, cover the pan and simmer until the chicken is cooked.

2nd Pan – Fry for 2 or 3 minutes (but do not brown) in a dessertspoonful of ghee or other fat, 1 sliced onion, and 1 or 2 cloves of garlic, sliced lengthwise. Now turn the contents of the first pan into the second. Salt and lemon juice to taste. Bring to the boil and simmer for 5 or 6 minutes.

Gram Pepper Water (*Koloo Tunny*)

1.1 l (1 quart) of gram water, *i.e.*, water in which the Southern India gram (koolthee) has been boiled.

Fry lightly in ghee or other fat a medium-sized onion and 2 cloves of garlic, finely sliced. Add to it:

1 teaspoonful of ground turmeric.
1 saltspoonful of ground chillies, together with 3 or 4 fresh green chillies, cut lengthwise in halves.

Now add the gram water and a dessertspoonful of thick tamarind pulp. Salt to taste. Bring to the boil before serving.

XXIV

Sundry Dishes

THESE dishes are not as a rule purely Indian. The influence of the cuisine of the West is very marked, but as they are largely consumed by Europeans and their descendants in India and are everyday dishes in their households, they are interesting, and will serve to vary the menu of ordinary homes.

Moglai Chops

6 lean lamb or mutton chops marinaded for an hour or more in the following mixture:

2 teacupfuls of Dhye (sour curds).
1 dessertspoonful of ground corianders or 1 teaspoonful of green corianders, minced.
1 dessertspoonful of ground Kus Kus (poppy seeds).
½ teaspoonful of ground chillies.
1 small saltspoonful of ground allspices.
1 pinch of ground cardamoms.
1 pinch of ground cloves.
A 12 mm (½ inch) piece of fresh or
    pickled green ginger   } minced finely.
2 cloves of garlic
Salt to taste.

Fry in a *sauté* pan ghee or other fat the chops and marinade in until the meat is well cooked. Then sprinkle over them a dessertspoonful of Chenna flour (Bengal Gram). Toss lightly for 2 or 3 minutes and serve.

Moglai Chicken

1 chicken prepared as for roasting, but the legs must be slightly scored. Marinade the chicken for an hour or more in the following mixture:

2 teacupfuls of Dhye (sour curds).
1 dessertspoonful of ground corianders.
½ teaspoonful of ground chillies.
1 saltspoonful of ground allspice.
½ teaspoonful of ground turmeric.
1 saltspoonful of ground cinnamon.
1 pinch of ground cardamoms.
2 cloves of garlic
A 25 mm (1 inch) piece of fresh or } minced
   pickled green ginger   finely.
Salt to taste.

Rub the marinade well into the chicken.

The chicken can either be roasted or baked. When half cooked, sprinkle with Chenna flour and baste well.

Moglai Leg of Mutton or Lamb

Score slightly as for a leg of pork and rub well into it a marinade similar to that for Moglai chicken and roast or bake in the same way.

Madras Buffath of Fresh Meat

450 g (1 lb) or more of beef cut in fairly thick slices, just covered with cold water and simmered, and when half cooked, 2 or 3 potatoes cut in halves, 2 or 3 carrots cut in halves, and 8 or 12 whole spring onions are added to it and cooked but not pulped.

Fry lightly in 56 g (2 ozs) of ghee or other fat for 3 or 4 minutes:

1 onion
1 clove of garlic } minced.
1 dessertspoonful of ground corianders.
1 teaspoonful of ground turmeric.
½ teaspoonful of ground cummin seed.
½ teaspoonful of ground mustard seed.
¼ teaspoonful of ground fenugreek.
½ teaspoonful of ground chillies.
4 green chillies, cut lengthwise in halves.

Then add the meat and vegetables and as much of the liquor as is required. Salt to taste and simmer for another few minutes before serving.

Madras Buffath of Cold Meat and Cooked Vegetables

Fry lightly in 56 g (2 ozs) of ghee or other fat for 3 or 4 minutes:

1 onion
1 clove of garlic } finely minced.
4 fresh or pickled chillies, cut in halves.

Then add 1 tablespoonful of curry powder or a tablespoonful of curry paste. Mix and continue the cooking for a few minutes longer. Gradually stir into it enough water to form a thick sauce, then add 450 g (1 lb) of cold meat cut up in thick slices and cold cooked potatoes, and any other vegetable (but not greens), sufficient for the amount of meat used. Add salt to taste, a teaspoonful of tamarind pulp and about 2 tablespoonfuls of thick cocoanut milk. Simmer gently until the meat is warmed through.

Mussala Beef Steak

Make a thick paste of the following ingredients:

1 dessertspoonful of ground corianders.
½ teaspoonful of ground cummin seed.
½ teaspoonful of ground mustard seed.
½ teaspoonful of ground turmeric.
½ teaspoonful of ground red chillies, with a sufficiency of vinegar.
Salt to taste.

The steak is prepared in the usual way, but thoroughly rubbed on both sides with this paste, and then fried in a little ghee or other fat until nearly done. Then add to the pan a tablespoonful of thick tamarind pulp and a little water. Simmer gently until the steak is cooked.

Mussala Beef Steak

(Another way)

Make, with a sufficiency of vinegar, a paste of the following ingredients:

½ teaspoonful of ground chillies.
½ teaspoonful of ground cummin seed.
1 teaspoonful of ground turmeric.
½ teaspoonful of ground mustard seed.
A little salt.

Rub the beef steak on both sides with this mixture, and either grill or fry in the usual way.

Mussala Mutton Chops and Cutlets

Mutton chops or cutlets or thick slices from a leg of mutton are treated and cooked in the same way as Mussala Beef Steak.

Mussala Fry (Beef Fry)

450 g (1 lb) of lean beef, cut up into 50 mm (2 inch) squares 12 mm ($\frac{1}{2}$ inch) thick.

1 onion
2 cloves of garlic   } chopped
2 fresh or pickled chillies   finely.
6 slices of fresh or pickled green ginger

1 tablespoonful of ground corianders
1 teaspoonful of ground turmeric
$\frac{1}{2}$ teaspoonful of ground cummin seed   made into
1 dessertspoonful of ground poppy   a paste
seeds or ground almonds   with a
$\frac{1}{2}$ teaspoonful or less of ground chillies   little
1 tablespoonful of freshly scraped   vinegar.
cocoanut

Fry lightly in the ghee for 2 or 3 minutes the chopped ingredients, then add the paste made with the other ingredients.

Mix well, and continue the frying for 3 or 4 minutes longer. Add the meat, cook for a few minutes longer with the pan uncovered. A thickish gravy will then appear. Now cover the pan closely and simmer until the meat is tender. Salt to taste.

Liver Fry

450 g (1 lb) of sheep's, lamb's or calf's liver, cut in slices 12 mm ($\frac{1}{2}$ inch) thick, well washed and dried.

With a very little vinegar make a paste of :

1 heaped teaspoonful of ground turmeric.
A generous pinch of ground chillies.
A generous pinch of ground black pepper.
A generous pinch of ground ginger.

Rub this into the liver on both sides. Now fry the liver in the ordinary way, and for gravy, using the fat in which the liver has been cooked, fry in it an onion and a clove of garlic, sliced finely, and 2 fresh or pickled chillies, cut lengthwise. Do not brown the onions.

Add a dessertspoonful of tamarind pulp and salt to taste. Let it warm through thoroughly and serve. If too thick, thin down with a little water.

Chilli Fry

450 g (1 lb) of any kind of meat cut up into convenient pieces.
1 tablespoonful of ghee, oil or other fat.
1 tablespoonful of sliced onions.
1 or 2 cloves of garlic, very finely sliced.
1 teaspoonful of ground cummin seed.
1 teaspoonful of ground turmeric.
1 teaspoonful of ground ginger.
$\frac{1}{2}$ teaspoonful of ground chillies, or 4 red or green, fresh or pickled chillies.
1 tablespoonful of tamarind pulp.
Salt to taste.

Cook the onions and garlic in the fat for 3 or 4 minutes, then add all the other ingredients except the meat and tamarind pulp, and cook on a slow fire for 5 minutes or so. Now add the meat. Stir thoroughly, cover the pan and cook slowly for an other 5 or 10 minutes, then add a small teacupful of water, cover the pan closely and simmer until the meat is cooked. Lastly, add the tamarind pulp. Stir and serve.

The chilli fry must have only a very little thick gravy.

Chilli Fry

(Another way)

Fry a sliced onion in a dessertspoonful of fat until a light brown. Then add 450 g (1 lb) of any kind of meat cut up in convenient pieces, and fry it for 3 or 4 minutes longer with the pan closely covered. Shake the pan occasionally.

Now add:

6 or 8 slices of green ginger.
2 green chillies.
2 dry red chillies, cut lengthwise.
6 or 8 spring onions.
1 clove of garlic, sliced finely.
1 dessertspoonful of tamarind pulp.

Add a teacupful of water. Simmer gently until the meat is tender. Salt and pepper to taste. The gravy must be thick.

Chilli Fry with Mussala

450 g (1 lb) of beef or mutton cup up into convenient pieces and fried in a little ghee or fat until slightly brown.

Remove the meat and in the same fat fry:

1 onion, sliced finely.
1 or 2 cloves of garlic, sliced finely.
2 chillies, fresh or dried.
½ teaspoonful of ground ginger.
½ teaspoonful of ground cummin seed.

Add the meat and half a teacupful of water and simmer very gently until the meat is tender. Now add 1 dessertspoonful or more of tamarind pulp and salt to taste. The gravy must be very thick.

Madras Fried Fish

Make a pickle of:

1 egg.
A teaspoonful of ground turmeric.
¼ teaspoonful of ground chillies.
A tablespoonful of finely chopped onions.
A clove of garlic minced finely.
Salt to taste.
Juice of ½ a small lemon.

Lay fillets or cutlets of fish flat in the pickle for half an hour or longer, turning them every now and again so that both sides are well covered with the pickle. Fry (without wiping) in boiling fat, enough to cover them. When sufficiently cooked remove, drain and serve, garnished with a sprig of parsley and slices of lemon.

Indian Fried Fish

Any sort of fish can be used.
Clean, wash and dry the fish and rub thoroughly into every portion of it a paste made with:

2 parts of ground turmeric.
1 part of ground chillies.
A little vinegar and salt.

Egg, breadcrumb and fry in the usual way.

Indian Batter for Frying Fish

Make the batter in the ordinary way and stir into it finely chopped onions, minced fresh or pickled chillies and a pinch of ground chillies, turmeric and salt.

Indian Stuffing for Fish

2 tablespoonfuls of minced onion.
1 clove of garlic, finely minced.
2 fresh or pickled chillies, finely minced.
1 dessertspoonful of chopped green coriander leaves.
1 teaspoonful of ground turmeric.
½ teaspoonful of ground cummin seed.
½ teaspoonful of ground ginger.

Fry the above ingredients in a little ghee or oil for 4 or 5 minutes, then add to it 2 tablespoonfuls of breadcrumbs and salt to taste. Blend thoroughly, and use in the usual manner as a stuffing for any kind of fish. If desired bind with egg.

Rice and Fish Rissoles

These are made exactly as the rice and meat cutlets (see p. 163), but a little ground turmeric and ground cummin seed is added to and cooked with the other ingredients.

Any kind of fish flaked, skinned and boned can be used for this purpose. Fish roe can also be used. Shape into rissoles, egg, breadcrumb, and fry in the usual way. Serve with chilli or chutney sauce.

Indian Fish Stew

Any kind of fish.
Fry lightly in sufficient ghee or oil:
1 onion
2 cloves of garlic } sliced finely.

2 or 3 red green fresh or pickled chillies.

2 or 3 red or green fresh or pickled chillies
½ teaspoonful of ground ginger.
1 teaspoonful of ground turmeric.

Add to this 1 tablespoonful of tomato puree or 225 g (½ lb) of whole tomatoes, skinned, and a teacupful of water. Salt to taste. Bring to the boil. Add sufficient fish for the amount of sauce. Cover the pan, shake it occasionally and let it simmer gently, until the fish is cooked.

Kedgeree

Cold cooked fish (flaky fish preferable).
Cooked Patna rice.
Butter.
Chopped onions.
A finely sliced clove of garlic.
Ground turmeric.
Hard-boiled eggs.
Pepper.
Salt.
Green and red chillies.

Cook in sufficient butter for a few minutes (but do not brown) the onions and garlic. Then add a teaspoonful of ground turmeric, and cook this mixture for 2 or 3 minutes longer.

The rice and flaked fish are now added and the whole very lightly tossed together until warmed through. Pepper and salt to taste.

Serve piled on a dish and garnished with slices of hard-boiled eggs and green and red chillies cut lengthwise.

Tamarind Fish or Pudda

1.4 kg (3 lbs) of any suitable kind of fish cut in slices or cutlets about 12 mm (½ inch) thick covered with plenty of salt and stood aside for 24 hours. Turn the cutlets two or three times so that the fish is well salted.

Cover 450 g (1 lb) of tamarind with about 1.1 l (1 quart) of good malt vinegar and let it soak for 5 or 6 hours. Then macerate it thoroughly, squeezing all the pulp out of it and getting the pulp as free from seeds and fibres as possible by passing it through a coarse sieve.

56 g (2 ozs) of ground chillies ⎫
28 g (1 oz) of ground turmeric ⎬ made into a thickish
14 g (½ oz) of ground ⎭ paste with
   cummin seed   vinegar.

113 g (4 ozs) of fresh or pickled green ginger ⎫ finely
28 g (1 oz) of garlic   ⎬ sliced.

Remove the fish from the brine and wipe each piece thoroughly dry, then rub both sides of the fish with the curry paste. Pour into a wide-mouthed jar sufficient tamarind pulp to cover the bottom. Then scatter over it a few pieces of the ginger and garlic, place a piece of fish on top of this and scatter a little more garlic and ginger on it, and then cover it with a layer of tamarind pulp. On this sprinkle a little more garlic and ginger, then pack on it another slice of fish and proceed as before until the jar is well packed. If any of the ingredients are left over, pack them well into the jar and add enough fresh vinegar to cover the lot. Hermetically seal the jar and stand it in the sun daily for 2 or 3 weeks. Shake the jar as often as possible during this time.

To Cook – Fry the desired quantity in ghee when wanted, and keep the jar well covered.

Tamarind Fish

Salt fish of any kind cut up into convenient pieces and washed in vinegar then drained and dried thoroughly.

Make a pickle of:

2 tablespoonfuls of ground corianders.
1 tablespoonful of ground turmeric.
1 dessertspoonful of ground chillies.
1 teaspoonful of ground ginger.
6 or 8 cloves of garlic, finely sliced.

With the liquor obtained by macerating 225 g (½ lb) of tamarinds in 570 ml (1 pint) of vinegar and straining in a coarse sieve or tammy, mix the pickle thoroughly, add the dried salt fish to it, pack into jars with closely fitting lids. This fish can be utilized in a fortnight.

To Cook – Warm ghee or other fat in a frying pan and fry the fish in it.

Ballachong (*Pickled Prawns*)

450 g (1 lb) prawns either fresh or bottled, pounded into a paste.

1 dessertspoonful of coarsely pounded dry red chillies.

1 dessertspoonful of fresh green ginger, peeled and finely chopped.

1 teaspoonful of finely chopped garlic.

2 tablespoonfuls of thick tamarind pulp, obtained by using vinegar.

Salt to taste.

570 ml (1 pint) or more of either gingili or mustard oil.

Put the oil to boil and then add all the other ingredients to it. Mix thoroughly and keep on stirring it till the oil begins to clear.

Prawn Ballachong

Mix together with a little vinegar:

1 dessertspoonful of ground turmeric.

1 teaspoonful of ground pepper.

1 teaspoonful of ground cummin seed.

1 teaspoonful of ground chillies.

In 570 ml (1 pint) of mustard or gingili oil, fry:

3 tablespoonfuls of finely chopped onions.

1 heaped teaspoonful of finely sliced garlic.

2 heaped teaspoonfuls of fresh or pickled ginger (minced finely).

6 or 8 fresh or pickled chillies, chopped finely.

Add the paste, mix well, simmer for a few minutes, and then add to it a sufficiency of fresh, canned or bottled prawns, chopped coarsely. Salt and lemon juice to taste.

When perfectly cold this pickle can be bottled and will keep for days if securely corked.

Chilli Fry of Dried Bombay Duck

½ dozen Bombay ducks cut across in halves.

1 large onion
2 cloves of garlic } finely sliced.

3 chillies, fresh or pickled, cut lengthwise.

1 teaspoonful of ground turmeric.

1 teaspoonful of ground ginger.

1 dessertspoonful of ground corianders.

Ghee or oil.

1 dessertspoonful of tamarind pulp.

Salt.

Fry slightly in sufficient ghee or oil in a deep frying pan the onions, garlic and chillies. Then add the ground corianders, turmeric and ginger. Fry for a minute or two, and add to it the tamarind pulp, and if too thick a little water.

Place the Bombay ducks in the pan. Shake occasionally, and simmer gently for 10 to 15 minutes. Any other kind of salt fish can be treated in the same way.

Tamarind Fry

450 g (1 lb) of any kind of fresh meat or liver cut up into rather large pieces.

Fry lightly in 56 g (2 ozs) of ghee or other fat for 2 or 3 minutes:

2 onions
2 cloves of garlic } minced finely.
4 fresh or pickled chillies

Then add the meat and after a few minutes of slow frying add about a teacupful of tamarind water and salt to taste. Cover the pan closely and simmer gently until the meat is tender.

Jhal Fry

225 g ($\frac{1}{2}$ lb) of cold meat of any kind, freed from skin and fat, and cut up into 12 mm ($\frac{1}{2}$ inch) dice.
28 g (1 oz) of ghee, butter, oil or fat of any kind.
2 tablespoonfuls of onions } minced finely together.
1 clove of garlic
$\frac{1}{2}$ teaspoonful of ground cummin seed.
$\frac{1}{2}$ teaspoonful of ground turmeric.
$\frac{1}{2}$ teaspoonful of ground red chillies.
$\frac{1}{2}$ teaspoonful of ground ginger.
1 tablespoonful of very thick tamarind pulp.
Salt to taste.

Cook the onions and garlic in the fat for 2 or 3 minutes, then add the cummin seed, turmeric, ground chillies and ginger. Stir thoroughly, add the meat and let it warm through gradually, adding, if necessary, a very little stock or water to prevent it catching. Add salt to taste, and lastly the tamarind pulp.

To Pickle Beef (*Anglo-Goanese*)

Cut 910 g (2 lbs) of beef, freed from skin and fat, into fairly large but convenient pieces. Rub each piece well with salt, and let it lie in the brine for 24 hours. Then press the brine out of it and rub each piece thoroughly with a paste made with vinegar of the following ingredients:

12 dry red chillies, coarsely pounded.
1 tablespoonful of ground turmeric.
1 tablespoonful of ground turmeric.
1 teaspoonful of ground cummin seed.
1 teaspoonful of ground mustard seed.
½ teaspoonful of ground ginger.

Now pack a layer of the prepared meat in a stone jar and lightly sprinkle over it a little finely chopped garlic and a few peppercorns, then another layer of meat, garlic, peppercorns and so on, until the jar is full. Cover closely with a close-fitting lid. Shake the jar occasionally and in 3 or 4 days the pickle is usable.

To Cook – Fry the meat in ghee or other fat.

Tholtee or Ding Ding (*Indian Biltong*)

This is meat – usually beef or venison – freed from fat and skin, cut into strips 150 mm (6 inches) long and about 25 mm (1 inch) thick, rubbed with salt, allowed to dry and then rubbed thoroughly with a mixture of:

2 parts of ground turmeric.
1 part of ground red chillies.

laid on mats or more often hung on strings in the sun until thoroughly dried. This is stored away and will keep for weeks.

When required the Ding Ding is hammered flat and either roasted on hot embers or fried in fat.

Ding Dings were largely used in the days when facilities for travelling were very difficult and days or even weeks were spent on journeys.

Tholtee or Ding Ding (*Indian Biltong*)

(Alternative)

Strips of meat 75 or 100 mm (3 or 4 inches) long and about 25 mm (1 inch) or more wide, thoroughly rubbed with a paste made with vinegar of ground turmeric, ground chillies, ground cummin seed, ground pepper, ground mustard seed and salt.

The strips are then either hung out or set out in the sun to dry thoroughly, and are then stored away for use as required.

The paste made as above can be used for devilling beef steaks or mutton chops.

Mutton or Beef Stew

1 tablespoonful of ghee or other fat.
910 g (2 lbs) of mutton beef, freed from skin and fat.
1 large onion, sliced.
1 clove of garlic, finely chopped.
4 Koffree chillies (Pepperoni or Sweet Peppers) cut length-
    wise in halves.
2 red or green or pickled chillies (cut lengthwise).
A generous pinch of black pepper.
2 cloves.
A 12 mm (1 inch) stick of cinnamon.
Salt.

Fry lightly for about 5 minutes in the fat, the onions, garlic, cinnamon and cloves. Then add the meat cut up into convenient sizes, the Koffree chillies and the other chillies. Mix lightly, cover the pan and let the meat stew gently in its own juice for 10 or 15 minutes. Then add just sufficient water or stock to form a thickish gravy and simmer until cooked.

If by chance the gravy is too thin, it must be allowed to eva-porate, or thicken it with a little flour. Now add pepper, salt, and vinegar to taste.

Chicken Stew

Joint the chicken into convenient pieces. In a little fat fry lightly for 3 or 4 minutes:

1 large onion
1 clove of garlic   } sliced finely.
2 fresh or pickled chillies

Then add to it:

2 cloves.
2 whole cardamoms.
A 12 mm (1 inch) stick of cinnamon.
½ teaspoonful of ground ginger.
A generous pinch of chopped mint.
A pinch of black pepper.

And continue the frying for another minute or two.

Now add the jointed chicken and sufficient water or stock in which it can simmer until tender. Salt and lemon juice to taste. Do not make the gravy watery, but should it be so, thicken with flour.

Duck stew is made in the same way, except that less fat and more chillies are used.

Pork Stew (*Goanese*)

910 g (2 lbs) of pork (any part) cut up into convenient sizes.

1 tablespoonful of fat.

1 large onion
2 or 3 cloves of garlic } finely sliced.

3 or 4 fresh or pickled chillies, cut in halves.

2 dry red chillies, cut in halves.

1 teaspoonful of ground turmeric.

½ teaspoonful of ground cummin seed.

½ teaspoonful of ground ginger, or 6 slices of green or pickled ginger.

½ teaspoonful of ground black pepper.

3 tomatoes chopped up or a tablespoonful of tomato paste or purée.

2 cloves.

A 12 mm (1 inch) stick of cinnamon.

2 whole cardamoms.

Fry in the fat for 4 or 5 minutes the onions, garlic, chillies, cloves, cinnamon and cardamoms. Then add the turmeric, cummin seed, ginger and pepper which should be previously mixed into a thick paste with a little vinegar.

Add the pork and lastly the tomatoes. Thoroughly mix with the other ingredients, cover the pan and let the contents simmer in their own juice on a slow fire until the meat is cooked. Salt and lemon juice to taste. If carefully cooked this dish will not need the addition of stock or water to form its gravy which should be thick and rich.

If too rich, remove some of the fat and add a little flour and water.

Indian Vegetable Stew

56 g (2 ozs) of ghee or other fat.

1 large onion ⎫
1 clove of garlic ⎬ thinly sliced.

1 large carrot (gajur) ⎫
1 small turnip (sulgum) ⎬ cut in 12 mm (1 inch) cubes.
2 large potatoes (aloo) ⎭

3 large tomatoes, chopped, or 1 dessertspoonful of tomato paste or purée.

1 dry red chilli or 2 or 3 fresh or pickled chillies.

3 thin slices of green ginger.

Salt to taste.

Fry in the ghee or other fat until a light brown, the onions and garlic. Then add the chillies, ginger and tomatoes and fry for a further 3 or 4 minutes. Add the carrots and turnips and 285 ml (½ pint) of water. Continue the cooking until these are nearly done. Now add the potatoes, salt to taste, and simmer until all are cooked. This stew should need no thickening.

When in season, the addition of green peas, scarlet runners, etc., are a great improvement. Various Indian vegetables are cooked in the same way.

XXV

Brinjals—(Aubergine)—Byngun

THIS vegetable hardly needs an introduction, for of late years its importation into England has increased so considerably that it is now obtainable in the season even at suburban greengrocers.

The Aubergine as known in England is either of the purple or black variety and elongated in form, but in India they are to be had round or long and varying in colour.

There are many ways in which this vegetable is utilized, either by itself or in combination with other food products as will be seen under the various headings.

Brinjal Mussala Cutlets

Parboil the brinjals and cut them in halves lengthwise. Remove some of the pulp, without breaking the skins.

In a dessertspoonful of ghee or other fat, fry lightly a small onion and a clove of garlic finely minced. Then mix into it:

    1 dessertspoonful of ground corianders.
    1 teaspoonful of ground turmeric.
    $\frac{1}{2}$ teaspoonful of ground cummin seed.
    $\frac{1}{2}$ teaspoonful of ground ginger.
    Less than $\frac{1}{2}$ teaspoonful of ground chillies.
    A pinch of pepper, and salt to taste.

Add now the pulp removed from the brinjals. Mix thoroughly, fill the skins, level the top, egg and breadcrumb them, and fry.

Brinjal Cutlets

3 medium-sized brinjals boiled until nearly cooked. Then cut them lengthwise in halves and scoop out as much of the inside pulp as possible without breaking the outer skins.

    A small onion
    A small clove of garlic
    2 green chillies   } very finely minced.
    6 thin slices of ginger

Fry these ingredients in a dessertspoonful of ghee or other fat.
Add 113 g ($\frac{1}{4}$ lb) of very finely minced cooked or uncooked meat of
any kind. Next add the brinjal pulp. Salt and pepper to taste.
Cook for 4 or 5 minutes if cold meat has been used, or longer
if the meat was uncooked.

Fill the brinjal skins with this mixture, level them at the top,
egg and breadcrumb, and either fry or bake.

N.B. – What is left over of the pulp can be formed into ordinary
rissoles and fried.

Brinjal Cutlet (*Vegetarian*)

The pulp scooped out of the brinjals is mashed and a slice of
stale bread which has been soaked in cold water and the water
squeezed out of it, is added, together with chopped onions,
a pinch of herbs, pepper and salt to taste.

The mixture is pressed into the skins, oiled over, egged,
breadcrumbed and baked or fried until brown.

Brinjal Cutlets

(Meat)

The filling is a blend of the pulp, soaked bread, chopped onions,
finely minced cooked meat of any kind, a pinch of herbs –
preferably mint only – pepper and salt to taste.

Baked or fried.

Brinjal Cutlets

(Fish, Prawns, Crabs or Lobster)

These are made similarly to the meat cutlets, but instead of the
mixed herbs, minced parsley is usually used.

Baked or fried.

Savoury Brinjal Cutlets

(With or without Meat)

The filling is a blend of the pulp and soaked bread, chopped
onions, preferably spring onions, a suspicion of garlic, minced
fresh green or pickled ginger, green or pickled chillies or ground
chillies, pepper and salt to taste, and minced meat of any sort
if required.

Brinjal Bake

Bake the brinjals until soft. Peel and pulp them with a tablespoonful of ghee or butter. Add to the pulp a tablespoonful of finely chopped onions, preferably spring onions, 1 or 2 green chillies chopped finely or a pinch of ground chillies, and salt to taste. Turn into a pie dish, sprinkle over with breadcrumbs, place one or two lumps of butter over it, and bake until brown.

Fried Brinjal

Cut the brinjal lengthwise in fairly thick slices, sprinkle salt over them, and in 5 minutes wash the salt off. Dry them with a cloth and then rub them on both sides with a paste made of:

2 parts of ground turmeric.
1 part of ground chillies.
A little vinegar.
Salt to taste.

Fry in ghee, oil or other fat, but not butter.

Fried Brinjals in Batter

Prepare the brinjals in the same manner as for ordinary fried brinjals, but let the slices be thinner, and before frying, dip in rather thick batter made in the usual way.

Brinjal Fry

An ordinary-sized brinjal.

Partially boil the brinjal. Remove the skin and cut it up into rather large pieces.

In about an ounce of ghee or other fat, fry lightly for a minute or two a heaped dessertspoonful or more of pepper water mixture. Toss the brinjal in this mixture. Do not pulp it. Salt to taste.

This is usually served with pepper water and rice.

Rice Batter for Brinjals

Make a batter in the ordinary way, using fine rice flour instead of ordinary flour.

Lady's Fingers (*Behndi – Bendikai*)

To Prepare – Dip them in boiling salt and water for 2 or 3 minutes and then scrape them to remove their excessive stickiness and stinginess.

Boiled Lady's Fingers (*Behndi*)

Prepare as above. Then boil them in fresh salted boiling water until tender. Drain thoroughly and serve with a squeeze of lemon juice over them and dusted with pepper. A sprinkle of either mustard, gingili or olive oil, is often added.

Fried Lady's Fingers (*Bendhi*)

Prepare and parboil the Behndis, then fry them in oil or ghee together with a finely sliced onion. Fry till crisp and brown. Flavour with ground chillies and salt.

Minced Cutlets

450 g (1 lb) of finely minced fresh meat of any kind.

1 onion
1 clove of garlic
A few fresh mint leaves   } all minced finely.
1 or 2 fresh or pickled chillies
1 12 mm ($\frac{1}{2}$ inch) piece of green ginger

Blend the meat with these ingredients, pepper and salt to taste, and bind the mixture with an egg. Shape into cutlets and fry a golden brown.

Cold meat can be used to make these cutlets, but a slice of bread soaked in water and the water well squeezed out of it will help to bind the mixture.

Chicken Cutlets

450 g (1 lb) of finely minced cooked chicken.

Fry in 28 g (1 oz) of ghee or other fat:

1 tablespoonful of spring onions
1 or 2 fresh or pickled chillies
6 thin slices of fresh or pickled   } minced finely.
   ginger
6 fresh mint leaves
$\frac{1}{2}$ teaspoonful of ground turmeric.

Pour off the excessive fat and blend these with the minced chicken, binding it with a slice of bread, which has been soaked and the water well squeezed out of it, and an egg.

If too soft, add a little flour and with floured hands shape into cutlets.

Egg, breadcrumb and fry a golden brown.

Sheep's and Lamb's Tongue Cutlets

Clean and soak the tongue in salt and water. Then cook gently until tender.

Skin and chop finely and blend with the same mixture as for Chicken Cutlets.

Brain Cutlets

To Clean – 2 sheep's or calves' brains.

These must be blanched, but before doing so, wash them well in cold salt water, and after removing the skins, fibres, etc., let them soak for an hour or two in fresh salt water.

To Cook – place them in sufficient cold water to which a little salt and vinegar has been added, and cook gently until firm. Drain and set to cool.

Then chop finely and blend in the same mixture as for chicken cutlets.

Potato Chops

Cold mashed potatoes blended with a little flour and egg.

In a dessertspoonful of ghee or other fat fry lightly:

An onion.
A small clove of garlic.
2 fresh or pickled chillies.

All finely chopped, add to it:

½ teaspoonful of ground ginger and
½ teaspoonful of chopped fresh mint.

Continue the frying for another 2 or 3 minutes. Finally add 225 g (½ lb) of finely minced cooked meat and just a little flour and milk to bind the mixture. Salt and pepper to taste.

Mix well and let the mixture cool.

Take a ball of the potato mixture and flatten it out with a cup-shaped depression in the centre which, fill with the meat mixture. Now cover with more of the potato. Flatten and shape into round cakes 50 mm (2 inches) in diameter. Egg and breadcrumb and fry until a golden brown. Drain thoroughly before serving.

N.B. – If preferred, bake the potato chops in a moderate oven. Any kind of cooked meat can be used.

Prawn Cutlets

1 large can of prawns	finely
1 medium-sized onion	minced
1 clove of garlic	and mixed
1 or 2 fresh green or pickled chillies	together.

Then blended with:

½ teaspoonful of ground ginger.
1 saltspoonful of ground chillies.
1 saltspoonful of black pepper.
1 teaspoonful of chopped mint.

Mix the whole together with a little breadcrumbs and an egg. Add salt to taste, and with lightly floured hands form into cutlets and fry in the usual way.

N.B. – Canned lobster, salmon and any kind of cooked fish can also be used to make these cutlets.

Prawn Cutlets

(Another way)

Mash the contents of a can of prawns and blend it with the following:

1 dessertspoonful of ground corianders.
1 teaspoonful of ground turmeric.
½ teaspoonful of ground cummin seed.
1 saltspoonful of ground red chillies.
3 fresh or pickled chillies.

1 small onion	finely minced.
1 small clove of garlic	

1 tablespoonful of fresh grated cocoanut or 1 dessertspoonful of finely desiccated cocoanut.
Salt to taste.

Bind the mixture with an egg and breadcrumbs, shape into cutlets with lightly floured hands. Fry in boiling ghee or oil.

These cutlets may be varied with the flavour of mint or parsley.

Canned lobster, salmon and any kind of cooked fish can also be used in this way.

Rice and Meat Cutlets

Mix together and thoroughly blend equal quantities of any kind of cooked minced meat and cooked rice into a paste. Sufficient onions, a small clove of garlic, green or pickled ginger, green chillies, either fresh or pickled, are minced together and fried in a little oil or ghee for 3 or 4 minutes.

Then add the blend of rice and meat and salt to taste. Mix thoroughly and set to cool. Form into cutlets and fry a golden brown and serve with chutney or chilli sauce.

Indian Stuffed Tomatoes

Six good-sized tomatoes. Remove part of the insides of even-sized, firm tomatoes, and blend with a little very finely minced cooked meat of any kind. Curry this as follows:

One small onion and 1 clove of garlic, finely minced and lightly fried in a very little ghee or other fat. A teaspoonful of curry powder or curry paste is added and cooked for 2 or 3 minutes. Then the minced meat and tomato are blended with it. Salt to taste. This mixture is then put into the tomatoes, which are now baked in a slow oven or very carefully fried without turning.

Any surplus mixture is easily converted into curry rissoles with a little flour, egg and breadcrumbs.

Fresh Tomato Sauce for Cutlets, etc.

450 g (1 lb) of tomatoes skinned and chopped.
1 clove of garlic ⎱
1 onion   ⎰ sliced finely.
A pinch of ground ginger.
A pinch of black pepper.
A pinch of ground chillies.

Put all these ingredients into a pan with sufficient water to form a thick pulp. Simmer gently until the tomatoes are quite soft. Add salt to taste and strain through a coarse strainer.

Tamarind Sauce

Prepare by macerating in cold water and straining 285 ml ($\frac{1}{2}$ pint) of thickish tamarind pulp. Add to it:

$\frac{1}{2}$ teaspoonful of ground ginger.
A generous pinch of ground chillies.
1 heaped tablespoonful of sugar.
A pinch of salt.

Simmer this mixture for 10 minutes. The sauce can be used with roast or stewed Pork, Duck, Goose, Veal, etc.

Goanese Fish Sauce

Fry lightly in a little ghee or butter:

1 onion   } finely sliced.
1 clove of garlic
A pinch of ground ginger.
A pinch of ground chillies.
$\frac{1}{2}$ teaspoonful of ground turmeric.

To this add 285 ml ($\frac{1}{2}$ pint) of fish stock and stir into it a well-beaten egg. Keep stirring it until the sauce begins to thicken. Then add salt and lemon juice to taste.

Vegetable Pickle

Prepare sufficient strong boiling brine. Have your vegetables cut into convenient sizes and drop them into the boiling brine. Then immediately remove the pan from the fire. In 5 minutes remove the vegetables from the brine and see that they are thoroughly well drained. Spread on perforated boards and thoroughly dry them either in the sun or before a fire.

Vinegar

(Use Distilled Vinegar)

To every 1.1 l (1 quart) of vinegar add 3 or 4 whole cloves, $\frac{1}{2}$ of a small teaspoonful of ground red chillies or capsicums, a clove of garlic, finely sliced, (25mm) an inch of green ginger well scraped, wiped dry, and cut into thin slices, add 3 or more fresh green or red chillies slit lengthwise and salt to taste.

Bring the vinegar with the ingredients gradually to the boil, then pour it over the dried vegetables. Let the pickle cool thoroughly, bottle and cork.

Indian Savoury Omelet

Two eggs well beaten, to which add 1 small onion and 1 green chilli very finely minced. Pepper and salt to taste, and if liked, a pinch of finely minced mint or mixed herbs.

Beat all together for a minute or two, then melt a dessert-spoonful of ghee or butter in an omelet pan. Pour in the mixture and cook slowly until the omelet is firm underneath. Then either fold the omelet in half and cook until done, or turn the omelet right over and cook on the other side.

Kofree Chillies – Sweet Peppers – Pepperoni

These chillies are to be had either more or less globular or elongated in form, and red, green or yellow in colour. In whatever dish they appear, or in whatever way they are cooked, they are most attractive.

Sweet peppers are to be had in many Eastern countries, also in America and in the south of Europe, and the cooking of them is more or less the same in all these countries.

The principal methods in India are:

(1) Use either whole or cut in halves as a vegetable in stews and curries.
(2) Cut in halves and fry.
(3) Stuff with various seasonings and either fry, *sauté*, or bake.

To prepare a chilli for stuffing:

With a pointed knife, carefully cut round the stem and remove the stalk to which there is a cluster of seeds attached. These seeds are blended with whatever filling you propose using. The stalk is utilized to close the gap after the chilli is filled. The seasonings are: Prawns, fish of any kind, minced meat, rice, vegetables, eggs, etc., all previously cooked and either curried or seasoned as desired.

Dried Chillies

24 large green chillies.
28 g (1 oz) of salt.
285 ml (½ pint) of Dhye.

Dissolve the salt in the Dhye, cut the chillies in halves length-wise, but not completely, and put them into the Dhye. Stand aside for 2 days, then remove the chillies from the pickle and set to dry. When partially dried they are put back into the pickle. Do this two or three times, and then dry them thoroughly and store them in this dry condition in jars.

To Cook. – Fry them until crisp, in ghee, oil or other fat.

Devilled Nuts

Any sort of nut can be used, but they must be decorticated.

Fry the nuts in butter, or preferably ghee, until a pale yellow. Drain, and whilst hot, toss them in a mixture of salt and cayenne pepper.

Pistachio, Cashew, Almonds and Ground Nuts are usually used in India.

Saioo—Moorkoo

SAIOO, Moorkoo, Moormoora, Patani, Choorvay, Chinnakonee, Iddy Hoppers, etc., are not usually made at home, but they are made and sold in the Bazaars.

Saioo and Moorkoo are made of rice flour, turmeric, chillies and salt in the form of a stiff batter which is passed through perforated ladles or moulds into deep boiling oil, the Saioo being much finer than the Moorkoo and is in lengths like ordinary fine Spaghetti. Moorkoo, on the other hand, is much thicker, and like curled Macaroni.

Moormoora, Choorvay, Patani, Cholum and other grains are usually sold parched or puffed, and may be plain or savoury in character. Chinnakonee is made of dried prawns finely powdered and blended with ground chillies and salt. It is eaten sprinkled over curry and rice, or, by the English, on bread and butter.

Iddy Hoppers are usually made by Mohammedans and hawked round early in the mornings, and eaten as a first meal with milk and sugar. A stiff batter of the mixture, which is made of rice flour and cocoanut milk, is pressed through tiny perforations on to a damp cloth, in the form of a network, lacy in appearance about 12 mm ($\frac{1}{2}$ inch) thick and the size of a tea-plate, and the Hopper is then placed on a cloth which is stretched tightly and tied over the mouth of a pot containing boiling water and steamed.

Boiled Drumsticks (*Mooroongakai*)

This vegetable is much appreciated by both rich and poor and is cooked in various ways, but principally in combination with meat and the pulses. It is often served as a plain vegetable on the tables of both English and Anglo-Indians, cut up in 75 mm (3 inch) lengths, tied in bundles of 6 or 8 pieces, boiled in salt and water until tender and drained thoroughly. Each piece is split open, and only the delicious inside is eaten.

Kulee

225 g (½ lb) of Raggie flour.
Salt.
570 ml (1 pint) of water.

Mix into a pint of cold water a dessertspoonful of Raggie flour
and a little salt. Bring rapidly to the boil, then add the rest of the
flour in a dry state, and, without mixing it, let it boil until the
flour tastes cooked.

Drain off the excess of water. Set the pan aside to cool a little,
and then, with a strong wooden spoon, mash it into a very stiff
dough. Form into large balls and serve with very hot vegetable
curries.

Kool

Kool is Kulee broken down into a gruel with sour milk.

Stewed Bombay Ducks

Cut the fish across in halves.

In a stewpan, fry lightly in oil, 1 large onion and 3 cloves of
garlic, minced finely, and add to it:

2 fresh or pickled chillies.
2 dry red chillies.
½ teaspoonful of ground cummin seed.
½ teaspoonful of ground turmeric.
1 tablespoonful of tamarind pulp.

Let these ingredients fry together for 4 or 5 minutes, then add
the Bombay duck and sufficient water to form a thick gravy.
Simmer for 10 to 15 minutes.

XXVI

Meetais, etc., Indian Sweetmeats and other Sweet Dishes

SWEETMEATS in India, with few exceptions, are eaten more or less as food for the nourishment of the body rather than as simple confections. The principal sweetmeats, such as the different kinds of Hulwas, Luddoos, Burfis, Coa, Dhood-Padah, Goolab Jamon, etc., etc., are usually professionally made by Halwais and Meetai Wallahs of all castes, and sold in the Bazaars or hawked in the streets, at fairs, and in railway stations, etc.

The substantial meetais are made of very rich and nourishing ingredients, such as ghee, malai, coa, dhood, soojee, shukker, badam, etc., and are consequently very sustaining. The making of these sweetmeats is much too complicated for the ordinary housewives who confine themselves to the making of such things as Poorees, Rotis, etc.

The recipes for sweets here given are, to an extent, westernized by the European races who have been in touch with India for the last few centuries, and are generally made by the ordinary native cooks.

Jellabies

With 450 g (1 lb) of flour and sufficient cold water, make a batter the consistency of thick cream and stand it in a warm place for 24 hours to ferment.

When ready, have a pan of deep boiling ghee or other fat, fill an ordinary small funnel (with your finger over the outlet) with the batter, and when your hand is right over the fat remove your finger and let the batter run into continuous double circles or figure 8's. Allow them to set, and turn them. They should be fried joined on to one another. When quite crisp and of a pale biscuit colour, separate and put them into the flavoured syrup, and you will find that the syrup will run through the pipes of the jellabies which will still remain very crisp. In 2 or 3 minutes take them out of the syrup and drain.

The syrup is made as follows:

910 g (2 lbs) of sugar.
1.1 l (1 quart) of water.
A few sprigs of saffron.
The inner seeds of 6 cardamoms

Boil until the syrup is rather heavy and keep warm.

Goolab Jamon

Broil each ingredient separately:

225 g ($\frac{1}{2}$ lb) of very fine soojee in 28 g (1 oz) of ghee.
113 g ($\frac{1}{4}$ lb) of dried milk in 28 g (1 oz) of ghee.
113 g ($\frac{1}{4}$ lb) of ground almonds in 28 g (1 oz) of ghee.

These ingredients must only be lightly broiled, on no account must they brown in the slightest.

Then mix all together with 2 or 3 eggs and knead until the dough can be formed into small rolls about 50 mm (2 inches) long and 12 mm ($\frac{1}{2}$ inch) diameter in the centre and tapering at the ends.

Fry in deep boiling fat, until a golden brown. Drain well and whilst hot drop them into a heavy syrup. They can either be eaten with the syrup or drained and rolled in castor sugar.

The syrup is made as for Jellabies, but instead of saffron flavour with rose essence.

Rasgollah

Turn 1.1 l (1 quart) of milk into Dhye or Tyre by bringing it to blood heat and then adding the juice of 3 lemons. When set, strain the curds through a coarse cloth. Tie the cloth and let the Dhye drain until it is almost dry.

Knead well, and you will then be able to form it into small balls the size of a large marble. Drop these into a rose-flavoured syrup (as for Goolab Jamon). Serve with the syrup.

Balashai

113 g ($\frac{1}{4}$ lb) of Chenna flour, broiled in 28 g (1 oz) of ghee.
113 g ($\frac{1}{4}$ lb) of ground almonds, broiled in 28 g (1 oz) of ghee.
113 g ($\frac{1}{4}$ lb) of dried milk, broiled in 28 g (1 oz) of ghee.

These ingredients must be broiled separately and lightly (not browned in the least), allowed to cool, and then mixed together into a stiff dough with 2 or 3 well-beaten eggs and the inner seeds of 6 cardamoms. Form into balls the size of walnuts and fry them a golden brown. Drop them whilst hot into a heavy rose-flavoured syrup for a few minutes. Then drain and roll them in castor sugar.

Meeta Pillau

450 g (1 lb) of Pillau or the finest Patna rice, well washed, soaked for 2 hours, and thoroughly drained.

225 g ($\frac{1}{2}$ lb) of ghee or butter.

6 cloves.

6 cardamoms.

Two 50 mm (2 inch) sticks of cinnamon.

$\frac{1}{2}$ teaspoonful of whole allspice.

113 g (4 ozs) of sultanas (kismis) ⎫

56 g (2 ozs) of blanched almonds ⎬ lightly fried in ghee.

56 g (2 ozs) of blanched pistachios or cashew nuts ⎭

$\frac{1}{2}$ teaspoonful of saffron, steeped in $\frac{1}{2}$ teacupful of warm water.

Sugar to taste.

Fry lightly in the ghee for 2 or 3 minutes the cloves, cardamoms, cinnamon and allspice, then add to it the rice and saffron. Toss lightly and continue the frying on a slow fire for 4 or 5 minutes longer. Now add sufficient boiling water to cover and stand an inch or two above the rice. Cover the pan closely and continue the slow cooking until the water is absorbed and the rice cooked. The sultanas and nuts are now lightly mixed into it, together with a little granulated or castor sugar or pounded sugar candy.

Savia

Savia is a manufactured article akin to coarse vermicelli. It is sold in the Bazars and is usually only obtainable during certain festivals or Eeds.

Utilizing coarse Italian or French Vermicelli, this dish is produced as follows:

Lightly broil 225 g ($\frac{1}{2}$ lb) of vermicelli and then place it in a *sauté* pan and just cover it with boiling water in which 56 g (2 ozs) of ghee or butter has been dissolved. Cover the pan and cook on a slow fire until the water has been absorbed and the vermicelli cooked. If the water added has been insufficient, a little more can be sprinkled on.

On no account stir this dish, but lift it lightly with a fork and toss it over. It will not stick to the pan if the heat is moderate.

Lightly mix into it – sultanas, pistachios and sliced almonds. Serve piled on a dish and garnished with freshly scraped cocoanut and dusted over with castor sugar. Malai (cream) is generally served with this dish.

N.B. – During certain Moslem festivities, it is customary to send your friends dishes of Savia generally prepared by the lady of the house and with pure gold or silver leaf as an additional garnish.

Chuckolee

225 g (½ lb) of Mydah (finest pastry whites) with pinch of salt in it.

56 g (2 ozs) of ghee or butter.

Rub the butter into the flour lightly and convert it into a dough with a little milk, or, if preferred, with an egg. Knead the dough until it is absolutely velvety to the touch and so pliable that it can be rolled out easily to the thickness of two pennies and cut into diamond shapes.

In a deep *sauté* pan bring gradually to the boil 170 ml (3 pints) of milk with two 50 mm (2 inch) sticks of cinnamon and 113 g (¼ lb) of sugar. When boiling, drop in, one by one, the pieces of dough and boil for 10 to 15 minutes with the pan uncovered. Remove the cinnamon and add 2 tablespoonfuls of thick cocoanut milk or cream (Malai).

This dish must be eaten as soon as it is cooked, or, like dumplings, the pastry will soon harden.

Flavours are varied according to taste, so instead of cinnamon, saffron or nutmeg is often used.

Madras Hulwa

The inner white part of the kernel of a fresh cocoanut, finely grated, *or* 4 tablespoonfuls of finely desiccated cocoanut.

1 heaped tablespoonful of poppy seeds

The inner seeds of 6 cardamoms.

225 g (½ lb) of soojee.

450 g (1 lb) of sugar.

113 g (¼ lb) of ghee.

The soojee and poppy seeds mixed together are broiled until a light brown, then mixed with the grated or desiccated cocoanut, sugar and cardamom seeds, with a pint of water stirred well into it, set to boil on a slow fire and stirred continually to prevent burning and until cooked.

The ghee is then gradually added to it and incorporated thoroughly into the mixture which is then turned on to flat tins and set to cool. Cut into fancy shapes.

Pastry for Pustholes – Samoosas or Poorees (Puffs)

> 450 g (1 lb) of Mydah (finest pastry white flour) with a pinch of salt in it.
> 113 g (4 ozs) of ghee or butter.

Lightly rub the ghee or butter into the flour and convert it into a dough by the addition of cold water or sour milk. Knead until you get it smooth and velvety.

Roll out the dough to twice the thickness of a penny, then stamp out circular pieces in sizes to suit your requirements, and on the centre of each piece place a sufficiency of whatever filling you have. Wet the edge of the pastry all round and turn one half over the other and press the edges down.

To cook – Fry in boiling ghee or other fat until they are a light golden colour on both sides. Be careful not to overcook them. If preferred, bake them.

Filling for Meeta Dhall Pustholes (Sweet Dhall or Lentil Puffs)

> 113 g (¼ lb) of Moosa Dhall or lentils (well washed).
> 4 whole cardamoms.
> 2 whole cloves.
> A 50 mm (2 inch) stick of cinnamon.

Boil the Dhall and spices in just sufficient cold water to cook the Dhall perfectly soft. If by chance you have any excess liquor, it must be poured away.

Warm an ounce of ghee or butter. Remove the spices and add the Dhall to the ghee, together with 2 tablespoonfuls of freshly scraped cocoanut or a like quantity of finely desiccated cocoanut. Sweeten to taste. Blend thoroughly. Cool down and use.

Filling for Meeta Naral Pusthole (Sweet Cocoanut Puffs)

225 g (½ lb) of freshly scraped or finely desiccated cocoanut.
6 cardamoms (inner seeds only).
56 g (2 ozs) of sultanas (kismis).
28 g (1 oz) of ground almonds.
113 g (¼ lb) of sugar.

All blended thoroughly together, and if desiccated cocoanut is used the mixture must be moistened somewhat with milk.

Filling for Meeta Kayla Pusthole (Sweet Banana Puffs)

Ripe bananas mashed with a fork and mixed with half its bulk of freshly scraped cocoanut or finely desiccated cocoanut. Sweetened to taste and flavoured with essence of rose.

Filling for Meeta Anna-Nas Pusthole (Sweet Pineapple Puffs)

Tinned pineapple will do. Pour away the syrup. Chop the pineapple, add half its bulk of freshly scraped or desiccated cocoanut. Sweeten to taste.

Pineapple Balls (Anglo-Indian)

2 eggs.
4 tablespoonfuls of sifted flour.
A pinch of salt.
Just enough milk to make a thick batter.

Add to it 4 dessertspoonfuls of pineapple cut up into very small dice. Mix lightly and drop a dessertspoonful of the mixture into deep boiling fat. When a golden colour, drain and serve immediately with castor sugar sifted over them.

If properly handled they should be very light and look like golden balls.

Instead of pineapple, other suitable fruit can be used.

Banana Fritters (Anglo-Indian)

Two large ripe bananas mashed into a pulp and added to a thick batter made with 113 g (¼ lb) of flour and 2 eggs, together with a little milk if necessary. Mix well and drop a dessertspoonful of the mixture into deep boiling fat. Cook to a golden brown, drain and serve well dusted with castor sugar.

Pootoo Rice

There are two kinds of Pootoo rice, namely, black and white. Both kinds are grown in Burma, not India, and are used for making sweet dishes. The rice is very glutinous and very nourishing.

White Pootoo rice is steamed until thoroughly cooked and served with freshly scraped cocoanut and granulated sugar or sugar candy.

Black Pootoo rice is not really black, but a deep purple in colour. It is ground into a fine flour which is used for making – with ghee, almonds, etc. – a rich sweetmeat called Tho-Thole.

Tho-Thole

This is a sweet dish more or less like ordinary Hulwa. It is made, however, with what is known as Black Pootoo rice flour, the other ingredients being sugar, ghee, thick cocoanut milk, and sliced almonds.

The sugar is formed into a thick syrup and to it is added the rice flour, cocoanut milk and the almonds, and, continually stirring the mixture, is boiled to a thick dough. The ghee is then gradually added and well blended with the other ingredients.

After a time the ghee will begin to separate from the bulk. This indicates that the Tho-Thole is cooked. It is turned out in flat pans, allowed to set and cool before being cut up into convenient pieces.

Pootoo Rice Fritters (*Anglo-Burmese*)

Convert into a very thick batter the following ingredients:

> 2 ripe bananas mashed into a pulp.
> 225 g ($\frac{1}{2}$ lb) of white Pootoo rice flour.
> 2 eggs.
> Thick cocoanut milk.
> Sugar to taste.

Drop spoonfuls of the batter into deep boiling fat and fry until a golden brown.

Pootoo Rice Balls

450 g (1 lb) of white Pootoo rice flour formed into a dough with a little water, kneaded well, and divided up into balls the size of a golf ball. Make a hole with your forefinger right through the centre of each ball and fill this with a mixture of freshly scraped cocoanut and castor sugar. Close the ends, round them off, and drop into boiling water. When cooked they will rise to the surface. Take them out, one by one, with a wire ladle and roll them in freshly scraped cocoanut.

If wanted particularly sweet, sprinkle castor sugar over them.

Rice Bread with Cocoanut

225 g ($\frac{1}{2}$ lb) of rice flour.
225 g ($\frac{1}{2}$ lb) of fresh cocoanut grated or 2 tablespoonfuls of desiccated cocoanut.
Sugar to taste.

This is made into a soft dough with hot water, kneaded thoroughly well, divided into balls, flattened out into a round cake with the hand and baked on a thoa or griddle.

Sweet Rice and Soojee Poorees

Lightly rub 113 g ($\frac{1}{4}$ lb) of butter or 56 g (2 ozs) of ghee into a blend of 225 g ($\frac{1}{2}$ lb) of wheat flour and 225 g ($\frac{1}{2}$ lb) of rice flour, and add the inner seeds of 6 cardamoms. Form into a firm dough with the addition of a little thick cocoanut milk or water. Roll out to 6 mm ($\frac{1}{4}$ inch) thickness and stamp out small round biscuits about 50 mm (2 inches) in diameter. Fry in deep boiling fat.

Have ready a warm rose-flavoured syrup, and when the poorees are cooked, drop them into the warm syrup for a few seconds. Then drain and sprinkle over with finely scraped fresh or desiccated cocoanut.

Soojee Poorees

These are made in the same way except that soojee flour is used instead of rice flour.

Rice Balls

Wash well 225 g (½ lb) of rice, and put it on to boil in 1.1 l (2 pints) of milk, together with 113 g (¼ lb) of white sugar and a 25 mm (1 inch) stick of cinnamon.

Simmer very gently until the rice is cooked, and has absorbed all the milk. Remove the cinnamon. Let it cool and when cold enough to handle, butter your hands lightly and make into small balls (about the size of a golf ball), then roll in freshly scraped or very fine desiccated cocoanut and serve with cream (Malai) and sugar.

Rice Pudding (Anglo-Indian Dish)

Wash well 2 tablespoonfuls of Burma rice and put it into a pie dish, together with 570 ml (1 pint) of milk, a dessertspoonful of butter, 3 tablespoonfuls of sugar and a small pinch of salt. Grate a little nutmeg over it and cook in a slow oven for 2 hours.

Rice Mould (Anglo-Indian)

113 g (¼ lb) of rice flour.
1.1 l (1 quart) of milk.
Sugar to taste.
Orange, lemon or almond essence.

The rice flour, mixed into a thin paste with a little of the milk, is added to the rest of the milk, which is first brought to boiling point. Sugar to taste is added, and stirring briskly, the mixture is boiled for about 20 minutes or until it attains the consistency of ordinary blancmange. The essence is now added and the mixture turned into a mould which has been rinsed well in cold water. When set, turn out of the mould and serve with cocoanut sauce.

Raggie Mould (Anglo-Indian)

This is made exactly the same way as rice mould, but Raggie flour is used instead of the rice flour.

Usually served with cocoanut sauce.

Soojee Mould (Anglo-Indian)

This is made in exactly the same way as Raggie or Rice mould, but very fine soojee flour is used instead of the Raggie or rice flour, and an ounce or two of chopped almonds is added.

Serve with cocoanut sauce.

Rice Congee (Southern India)

(Invaluable for Invalids)

Boil 113 g (¼ lb) of well-washed Patna rice to a pulp and pass through a very fine sieve. Then beat into it an egg and add sufficient milk to thin it down to the consistency of a gruel. Flavour with grated nutmeg or ground cinnamon, and add either sugar or salt to taste. Boil up before serving.

Rosa Cruickeese (Anglo-Indian)

This is a thin batter made of 113 g (¼ lb) of fine rice flour, 2 well-beaten eggs, a little castor sugar or very fine soft sugar, and a little thick cocoanut milk (from fresh cocoanut). The batter must be well blended or the frying mould will not take it up.

To cook, dip a frying mould into deep boiling fat to heat it thoroughly, then lift it from the fat, dip it into the batter and rapidly replace it in another pan also containing deep boiling fat, until it is light golden brown in colour. Then lift it out and shake it from the frying mould.

It is usual to have two moulds to work with. The moulds used are about 50 mm (2 inches) in diameter, 25 mm (1 inch) in depth, shaped like a rose with five petals – open top and bottom.

This batter can also be utilized for waffles, using the waffle iron.

Beveca (Anglo-Indian)

285 ml (½ pint) of very thick cocoanut milk extracted from 2 large fresh cocoanuts.
113 g (4 ozs) of rice flour.
170 g (6 ozs) of soft white sugar.
Essence of rose.

Convert the sugar into a syrup with a little water. Add to it the cocoanut milk and rice flour. Mix thoroughly and cook, stirring continuously until the mixture thickens. Flavour with essence of rose. Pour into a buttered dish and bake a light brown.

Beveca (Goanese-Southern Indian)

Extract from the grated inner white part of the kernel of a large fresh cocoanut a large teacupful of thick cocoanut milk by pouring this quantity of boiling water on the grated cocoanut and then, after letting it stand for 10 or 15 minutes, pressing the milk out of it.

Beat into this milk 225 g (½ lb) of castor sugar, 225 g (½ lb) of ground rice and 2 eggs, together with about 56 g (2 ozs) of blanched and sliced almonds. The mixture should now be fairly thin; if not, add a little more cocoanut milk and then boil, stirring continuously until it thickens to the consistency of a very thick batter. Pour into a buttered baking dish and bake for about 30 minutes.

Beveca (Anglo-Indian–Southern Indian)

1 teacupful of rice flour and 1 teacupful of ordinary flour (sifted together).
56 g (2 ozs) of almonds, blanched and sliced.
113 g (4 ozs) of butter.
4 eggs.
Thick cocoanut milk.
Carraway seeds.
225 g (½ lb) of castor sugar.

Cream the butter and sugar together, then add the eggs one at a time and gradually add the mixture of rice and flour, together with a few carraway seeds. Thin with thick cocoanut milk. Butter a baking tin, pour the batter into it, sprinkle over with almonds, and bake in a moderate oven until of golden hue. Turn out of the tin, cut up into fingers and serve.

Beveca (Anglo-Indian and Deccan)

This is exactly similar to the Southern Indian, except that instead of ground rice being used, soojee is used.

Soojee Kul Kuls

450 g (1 lb) of soojee.
3 eggs.
Thick cocoanut milk.
28 g (1 oz) of ghee or oiled butter.

Rub into the dry soojee the ghee or oiled butter, and convert it into a stiff dough with 3 eggs and sufficient thick cocoanut milk. Knead until pliable, then take pieces of the dough the size of a walnut, and with greased butter pats roll into scrolls. Drop these scrolls into boiling fat one at a time and cook to a golden brown. When thoroughly cool, drop them into a thick syrup so that they get entirely coated. Remove from the syrup and let them dry.

Kul Kuls or Kajoors

450 g (1 lb) of rice flour.
2 eggs.
Cocoanut milk.
1 level tablespoonful of ghee or butter.
38 g (1 oz) of sugar.
A pinch of salt.

Mix together the rice flour, sugar, ghee or butter and a pinch of salt, and convert into a dough with the eggs and just enough of very thick cocoanut milk. Make balls of the dough the size of a walnut, and using greased butter pats roll them into scrolls. Drop these scrolls into deep boiling fat one at a time, as they are sticky and liable to stick together. When slightly golden in colour, drain thoroughly and sprinkle liberally with sugar.

Kul Kuls will keep for weeks, but they must be thoroughly cooled and well sprinkled with castor sugar.

Panyarums

225 g (½ lb) of rice flour.
56 g (2 ozs) of ordinary flour.
1 egg.
2 or 3 bananas.
113 g (¼ lb) of soft brown sugar.

Make a stiff batter of the rice flour with the egg and a little warm water. Cover and stand aside in a warm place for an hour or more.

Pulp the bananas with the sugar and wheat flour and add this to the rice batter. Mix thoroughly and drop a tablespoonful into boiling fat and cook as fritters. If the batter is too thick, thin down with a little milk.

Rice Flour Aliathrum

225 g (½ lb) of rice flour.
113 g (¼ lb) of castor sugar.
1 level tablespoonful of ghee or butter.

2 eggs.
Milk.
A pinch of saffron.

Cream the ghee or butter and sugar together, stir in the rice flour, mix thoroughly, and add 1 egg at a time to make a stiff batter. Flavour with a pinch of saffron. If the batter is too stiff, thin down with a little milk.

Drop a tablespoonful of the batter into boiling fat and cook as ordinary fritters. Drain and serve with soft white sugar over them.

Soojee Aliathrum

This is made in exactly the same way as rice flour aliathrum, but very fine soojee flour is used instead of rice flour.

Flavour with the inner seeds of 2 or 3 cardamoms.

Rogni Roti

225 g (½ lb) of finest pastry whites   } sieved
225 g (½ lb) of soojee (fine wheat semolina) } together.
225 g (½ lb) of sugar   made
½ teaspoonful of saffron steeped in a ½   } into a
   teacupful of warm water   } syrup.
170 g (6 ozs) of ghee or butter.

Rub the ghee or butter lightly into the flour and convert into a dough with the syrup. Knead well and roll out to a 6 mm (¼ inch) thickness. Stamp out biscuits the size of coffee saucers and bake on both sides on a griddle.

Indian Cream (Malai)

This is made by reducing cow's or buffalo's milk to half its bulk by the continuous application of gentle heat. During the process the milk will become creamy in appearance. It must not, however, be allowed to discolour by any increased application of heat.

Kheer

570 ml (1 pint) of milk.
1 tablespoonful of ground rice.
Chopped almonds.

Chopped pistachios.
Thick cocoanut milk.
Sugar.

Bring the milk gradually to the boil and stirring continuously sprinkle in the ground rice, and when it begins to thicken add ground almonds, pistachios and sugar and flavouring, such as orange, rose, etc. Now add the cocoanut milk. The Kheer should be of the consistency of ordinary custard. If too thick, thin down with milk or cream.

Kheer is sometimes served decorated with pure gold and silver leaf.

Cocoanut Sauce or Custard (*Anglo-Indian*)

This is a custard sauce made in the ordinary way blended with very thick cocoanut milk.

Koykotay

450 g (1 lb) of rice flour.
113 g ($\frac{1}{4}$ lb) of brown sugar.
Cocoanut milk.

Mix the brown sugar and rice flour together, and with very thick cocoanut milk convert into a stiff dough. Form into balls the size of a walnut and steam them.

Koykotays in Southern India take the place of christening cakes amongst the Tamils.

Glossary

English	Hindustani	Tamil
ACID	KUTTA	PULPPU
ALLSPICE	KABAB CHEENE	VELLAI-MILAHU
ALMONDS	BADAM	VATHUMAI
ALUM	PHITCARI	PADIKARAM
ANISEED	SAUNF	VENDHYAM
APPLES	SAYOO	APPIL-PARAM
ASSAFOETIDA	HING	PERUNKAYAM
BANANAS	KAYLA	VARAIPPARAM
BARLEY	JOWARI	{ CHOLAM VARKOTHÜMAI
BEANS	SAME	AVARAI
BEEF	GHAI KA GOSHT	MADOO KARI
BEETROOT	CHUKUNDA	SINIKKIRANGU
BLACK PEPPER	KALA MIRCHI	MOLOO
BONE	HUDDI	ELUMBU
BRAIN	BHEYJA	MOOLAY
BREAD	ROTI	ROTI
BRINJALS	BYNGUN	KUTHERAKOI
BROWN SUGAR	SHUKUR	CHUKERAY
BUTTER	MUKHAN, MUSKA	VENNAY
BUTTER	GHEE	NAY
BUTTERMILK	GHOL	THYROO
CABBAGE	GOBEE	KEERAY
CARDAMOM	ELACHI	ELAM
CARROT	GAGUR	{ VENSIVAPPU- KIRANGU
CAULIFLOWER	PHOOLGOBEE	PUKKIRAI
CAYENNE PEPPER CHILLIES, RED	} LAL MIRCHI	MOLOOGAH
CHARCOAL	KOELA	NILA-KARI
CHICKEN	MOORGEE	KHOLEE COONGEE
CINNAMON	DHALL CHEENE	KARUVAPPADAI
CLOVES	LAONG	LAVUNGAM
COCOANUT	NARUL	THAINGAH
CORIANDERS	DHUNIAH	KOTHAMILEE
CREAM	MALAI	PALADAI
CUCUMBER	KHEERA	VELARIKKAI

English	Hindustani	Tamil
CUMMIN SEED	JEERA	CHEEREGUM
CURDS	DHYE	THYROO, TYRE
CURRY POWDER	MASALAH	MUSSAHLAY
CHILLI	MIRCHI	MOLOOGAH
DRIPPING	CHURBEE	KORUPPU
DRUMSTICK		MOOROONGAKOI
DUCK	BUDHUK	VATHOO
DRIED RED CHILLIES	SOOKA MIRCHI	MOOLAGA
DRIED GINGER	SONT	INGEE
EGGS	UNDAY	MOOTAY
FAT	CHURBEE	KORUPPU
FENUGREEK	METHEE	VENTHIUM
FISH	MUCHLEE	MEEN
FLOUR (Pastry Whites)	MYDAH	MAUVU
FOWL	MOORGEE	KHOLEE
GARLIC	LUSSON	VELLAYPOONDOO
GINGER, GREEN	UDRUK	INGEE
GOOSE	BURRA BUDHUK	PERRI VATHOO
GRAM	CHENNA	CUDDALAY
GREENS	BHAJI	KEERAY
GUINEA FOWL	BURRA TEETUR	GINI-KORI
HARE	KHARGOSH	MUYAL
HEAD	SIRR	THALAI
ICE	BURRUF	PANIKKATTI
INDIAN CORN	BHOOTA	CHOLUM
JAGGERY	GOOR	VELLUM
KIDNEY	GOORDA	PUKKAM
KNOL KHOL	GART GOBEE	NULKOL
LADY'S FINGERS	BEHNDI	BANDAKOI
LAMB	BUCKRA	AHTOO KOOTTEE
LEMON	BURRA NIMBU	YELLUMSHIKAI
LIMES	NIMBU	YELLUMSHIKAI
LIVER	KALEJA	EERAL
MACE	JAFFATRY	JAPATRI
MANGO	AM	MANGA
MARROW	GOODA	MOOLAY
MEAT	GOSHT	MAMISAM
MELON	KARBOOZA	PICHAIKKAI
MILK	DOODH	PAHL
MINT	POOTHEENA	PUTHINA
MUSTARD	RAI	KUDOO

English	Hindustani	Tamil
MUSTARD OIL	KURVA TEIL	KADUHENNAI
NECK	GHURDA	KARUTHU
NUTMEG	JAIPHUL	JATHIKKAI
ONION	PEAZ	VUNGIUM
ORANGE	NARRANGEE	KITCHELLY PULLUM
PARTRIDGE	BURRA TEETUR	KAVUDARI
PEAS	MUTTER	PATANI
PEPPER	KALA MIRCHI	MOLOO
PICKLE	ACHCHAR	OORUKAI
PIGEON	KABOOTHUR	PURRAH
PISTACHIOS	PISTACH	PISTACH-KOTTAI
PLANTAINS	KAYLA	VAWLEY PALAM
POMEGRANATE	ARNAR	MATHULAM PARAM
POPPY SEEDS	KUS KUS	KASAKASA
PORK	SOOWAR KA GOSHT	PUNNY
POTATO	ALOO	URULAIKKIRANGU
PRAWN	GINGA	YERRAH
PRESERVE	MOORABA	
PUMPKIN	KUDDOO	POOSANIKKAI
QUAIL	CHOTA BUTTER	
RABBIT	KHARGOSH	MUYAL
RADISH	MOLEE	MULLANGI
RAISINS	KISMIS	{ MUNTHIRI KAINDADRATCHAI
RIBS	SEENA	VILAVELUMBU
RICE	CHAWAL	ARACHEE
ROAST	KABAB	PORIAL
SAFFRON	ZUFFRON	KUNGUMAPPU
SALT	NEEMUCH	HOOPOO
SALT FISH	NEEMUCH MUCHLEE	KARAVHAT
SEMOLINA	SOOJEE	KOTHUMAI-RAVAI
SHEEP	BUCKRA	AHTOO
SHRIMP	CHOTA GINGA	CHINACONEE
SNAKE GOURD		PODLINGKAI
SNIPE	CHAHA	ULLANKURUVI
SOUP	SHOORVA	RASAM
SOUR	KUTTA	PULPPU
SPICES	GHURM MUSSALA	GHURMASALAH
SUGAR	CHEENEE	CHUCKERAY
SULTANAS	KISMIS	PERIA DRATCHAI
TAMARIND	IMLEE	PULEE
TOMATO	BELATEE BYNGUN	THUCKALEY

English	Hindustani	Tamil
TONGUE	JEEB	NAUKKU
TURNIP	SULGUM	KIRANGU
TURMERIC	HULDEE	MUNJAL
TYRE	DHYE	DHYE
VEGETABLES	THURKAREE	MARAKKARI
VEGETABLE MARROW	COMLONG	SORAKKAI
VENISON	HURAN KA GOSHT	
WATER	PANI	THUNNY
WILD DUCK	MOORHABI	VATTU
INDIAN LENTILS	CHENNA	CUDDALAY
	MOOSA or MUSSOR	
	TOOR	PURPOO
	MOONG	
	SOORTHEE	
	UDUTH or URED	OOLOONTHOO

I am greatly indebted to Mrs. Templeton, late of Madras and of Perkham Road, West Kensington and Mr. C. T. K. Pathy of the School of Oriental Studies, Westminster, for their assistance in compiling the Tamil section of this Glossary.

E. P. VEERASAWMY

Index

CURRY ADJUNCTS
Cocoanut Milk, 1st Method, 14
  2nd Method, 14
Cocoanut Paste for Curries, 14
Thick Tamarind Pulp, 15
Thin Tamarind Pulp or Water, 15
Dhye (Sour Curds), 15
Puppadums (to cook), 15
Bombay Ducks (to cook), 15

RICE
Treatment of Rice before Cooking, 16
Plain Boiled Rice, 16
Rice Cooked by Absorption, 17
Spicy Cocoanut Rice (Copra Kana), 17
Simple Cocoanut Rice (Copra Kana), 17
Cocoanut Milk for Cocoanut Rice 18
Savoury or Yellow Rice, 18
Savoury Rice or Cold Cooked Rice, 18
Rice and Spaghetti, 19
Kitcheree, 19
  (Plain), 20
To Reheat or Warm Up plain Boiled Rice, 20
To utilize Rice Water, 20
Savoury Rice for Garnishes or as a Vegetable or Entrée, 20

PILLAUS AND BIRIANIS
Moglai Biriani – Sections A, B, C, 22-4
Rice for Pillau, 24
Moorgee Kabab Pillau, 25
Kooftah Pillau, 25
Prawn Pillau, 26
Madras Prawn Pillau, 26
Deccan Mutton or Lamb Pillau, 26
Madras Mutton or Lamb Pillau, 26
Madras Chicken Pillau, 27
Vegetable Pillau, 28

KORMA
Duck Korma, 29
  Another way, 29
Chicken Korma, 30
  Another way, 30
  Another way, 31
  Another way, 31
Chicken Korma (for Pillau), 32
Mutton Korma, 32
Korma of Lamb or Mutton, 33
Mutton or Lamb Korma, 33
Koormah Curry, 34

KOOFTAHS
Kooftah Curry, 35
Madras Kooftah Curry, 36
Deccan Kooftah Curry, 36
Prawn Kooftah Curry, 37
  Another way, 38
Cold Meat Kooftah Curry, 39
Anglo-Goanese Kooftah Curry, 39

KABABS
Shikampooree Kabab, 41
Moglai Hoosaini Kabab (Spicy), 42
Sami Kabab (Spicy), 42
Moglai Sami Kabab (Plain), 43
Dry Hoosaini Kabab, 43
Devilled Kabab Curry, 44
Kooftah Kabab, 44
Marinade for Kababs, 45
Moglai Kabab, 45
Stick Kabab, 45
Plain Stick Kababs, 46
Goanese Stick Kabab, 46
Dry Kababs of Mutton and Pork, 46
Hurran ka Ghosht Kabab, 47

CHICKEN, DUCK AND GAME CURRIES
Chicken Curry (Ceylon), 48
Madras Chicken Curry, 48
Chicken Curry, 49
  Another way, 49

Chicken Curry—cont'd.
 Another way, 50
 Another way, 50
 Another way, 51
Hyderabad Chicken Curry (with
 Sliced Cocoanut), 51
Chicken Curry with Greens, 52
Chicken and Dhall Curry, 53
Chicken Curry with Chenna Dhall,
 53
Dry Chicken Curry, 54
Dry Curry of Cold Chicken, 54
Dry Curry of Cold Chicken, etc.,
 55
Cold Poultry or Game Curry, 55
Rabbit Curry, 55
Duck Curry, 56
Deccan Duck Curry, 56
Madras Duck Curry, 57
Duck and Green Pea Curry, 57
Wild Duck Curry, 58

MUTTON, LAMB, BEEF AND
PORK CURRIES
Stick Curry, 59
Madras Stick Curry, 59
 Another way, 60
Pork Curry, 60
Mutton or Beef Curry with Sour
 Curds, 61
Drumstick Curry, 61
Madras Mutton Curry, 62
Deccan Beef or Mutton Curry, 62
Beef Curry, 63
Madras Beef Curry, 63
Calcutta Beef Curry, 64
Beef and Dhall Curry, 64
Madras Dhall and Meat Curry, 65
Meat and Potato Curry, 65
A Cold Meat Curry, 66
Methee Bhagi Curry (Fresh Meat),
 66
Methee Bajee Curry (Cooked Meat),
 67
Minced Meat and Lettuce Curry,
 67
Mince Curry, 68

EGG, LIVER AND TRIPE
CURRIES
Madras Egg Curry, 69
 (Fish flavour), 69
Egg Curry, 69
Egg Curry with Brinjals, 70

Egg Curry with Green Peas, 70
Liver Curry, 70
Madras Liver Curry, 71
Dry Tripe Curry, 71
Tripe Curry, 71

DRY CURRIES
Devilled Poultry, 73
Chicken Country Captain, 73
 Another way, 73
 Another way, 74
Country Captain of Cold Meat, 74
Madras Dry Curry of Fresh Meat,
 74
Madras Dry Curry of Cold Cooked
 Meat, 75
Dry Curry, 75
Dry Curry of Cold Meat (Chun-
 dole), 76
Dry Mince Curry, 76
Dry Curry of Cooked Meat, 77

VINDALOOS
Pork Vindaloo, 78
 Another way, 79
Duck Vindaloo, 79
 Another way, 80
Beef Vindaloo, 80
 Another way, 81
 Another way, 81

FISH
Fish Curry, 83
 Another way, 83
Bombay Fish Curry, 84
Eels Curry, 84
Salt Fish and Tomato Curry, 85
Bombay Ducks or other Salt Fish
 and Brinjals, 85

PRAWNS
Madras Prawn Curry, 87
Prawn Curry, 88
Madras Dry Prawn Curry, 88
Dry Prawn or Lobster Curry, 88
Prawn or Lobster and Cucumber
 Curry, 89
Prawn and Egg Curry, 89
Prawn and Brinjal Curry, 90
Madras Prawn and Brinjal Curry,
 90

MOLEES
How to Prepare a Molee for
 General Use, 92

Fish Molee, 92
Fish Molee of Cooked Fish, 93
Prawn or Lobster Molees, 93
Chicken Molee, 94
Mutton or Beef Molee, 94
Duck Molee, 95
Brinjal Molee, 95
Egg Molee, 96

DHALLS
Bengal Dhall, 97
Dhall Curry, 98
    Another way, 98
Mogul Dhall Curry, 99
Dhall or Indian Lentil Curry, 99
Moosa or Mussoor Dhall Curry,
100
Fried Dhall, 100
Meeta Dhall, 101
    Another way, 101
    Another way, 101
Dhall with Brinjals, 102
Dhall with Spinach, 102
Dhall with Greens, 103
Dhall, 103
Dhall Rissoles, 104

VEGETABLE AND VEGETABLE
CURRIES (Chitchkee)
To Curry Uncooked Vegetables,
105
To Curry Cooked Vegetables, 106
Dry Vegetable Curries, 106
Vegetable Curry – Beans and
Potatoes, 106
Madras Vegetable Curry, 106
Mutchakotay – Haricot or Butter
Beans Curry, 107
Meeta Mutchakotay – Haricot or
Butter Beans Curry, 107
Dry Curry of Haricot or Butter
Beans, 107
Country Captain of Vegetables,
108
Ghota ka Bhagi, 108

FOOGATHS
Drumstick Foogath, 109
A Foogath of Beans, 110
Banana Foogath, 110
Behndi or Lady's Fingers Foogath,
110
Tomato Foogath, 111
Cabbage Foogath, 111

Carrot Foogath, 111
Mooroongalai Foogath, 112

BOORTHAS
Prawn Boortha, 112
Vegetable Marrow Boortha, 112
Pumpkin Boortha, 113
Tomato Boortha, 113
Cucumber Boortha, 113
Brinjal Boortha, 113
Behndi Boortha, 114

SAMBALS
Sambal Dressing, 115
Sambal Sauce, 115
Brinjal Sambal, 115
Prawn Sambals, 116
Lobster or Crab Sambal, 116
Tomato Sambal, 116
Potato Sambal, 116
    Another way, 116
Cold Potato Sambal, 117
    Another way, 117
Sambal of Mixed Vegetables, 117
Egg Sambal, 117
Prawn and Egg Sambal, 117
Fish Sambals, 118
Cold Chicken Sambal, 118
Butter or Haricot Beans Sambal,
118
Lady's Fingers Sambal, 118
Onion Sambal, 118
Banana Sambals, 118
Cocoanut Sambal, 118
Apple Sambal, 119

FRESH CHUTNEYS
Mint Chutney, 120
Cocoanut Chutney, 120
Tamarind Chutney, 121
Dhall Chutney, 121
Coriander Chutney, 121
Green Tomato Chutney, 121
Mooroongakai Chutney, 121

SAVOURY FRITTERS
(Bhugias, Poorees and Philouries)
Bhugias, 122
Prawn Bhugias, 122
Rice Bhugias, 123
Soojee Bhugias, 123
Philouries (Dhall Fritters), 124
Philouries (Soojee Fritters), 124

Dhall Kara Pooree (Hot Savoury Dhall Pastry), 124
Kara Vuddays, 125

PUSTHOLES and SAMOOSAS
Pastry for Pustholes and Samoosas, 126
Fillings for Pustholes and Samoosas, 126–7

CHUPATTIES, PARATTAS, ROTIS
Instructions for Baking Chupatties, etc., 128
Chupatties (unleavened Wheaten Cakes), 129
Sweet Chupatties, 129
Rice Flour Chupatties, 129
To prepare Rice Flour, 129
Jowari Roti or Chupatties, 130
Parattas (Deccan Wheaten Cakes), 130
Phoolkay, 130
Atta Roti, 130
Rice and Cocoanut Bread, 131
Madras Hoppers, 131
Raggie Roti, 132

SOUPS AND MULLIGATAWNY
To prepare Tamarind Water for Mulligatawny, Pepper Water, etc., 133
Mulligatawny, 133
Consommé Mulligatawny, 133
Mulligatawny (with ordinary Meat Stock), 134
Chicken Mulligatawny, 134
Chicken Mulligatawny (made with Mulligatawny Paste), 135
Chicken Curry Soup, 135
Mutton Mulligatawny, 135
Mulligatawny (with Vegetable Stock and Mulligatawny Paste), 136
Dhall Mulligatawny, 136
Dhall Mulligatawny (made with Mulligatawny Paste), 136
Dhall Purée, 137
Rice Soup, 137
Rice Purée, 137
Plain Pepper Water, 138
Another way, 138
Dhall Pepper Water, 139
Another way, 139
Another way, 139

Vegetable Pepper Water, 140
Fish Pepper Water, 140
Meat Pepper Water, 140
Pepper Water, 141
Chicken Pepper Water, 141
Gram Pepper Water, 141

SUNDRIES
Moglai Chops, 142
Moglai Chicken, 142
Moglai Leg of Mutton or Lamb, 143
Madras Buffath of Fresh Meat, 143
Madras Buffath of Cold Meat and Cooked Vegetables, 144
Mussala Beef Steak, 144
Another way, 144
Mussala Mutton Chops and Cutlets, 145
Mussala Fry, 145
Liver Fry, 145
Chilli Fry, 146
Another way, 146
Chilli Fry with Mussala, 147
Madras Fried Fish, 147
Indian Fried Fish, 147
Indian Batter for frying Fish, 148
Indian Stuffing for Fish, 148
Rice and Fish Rissoles, 148
Indian Fish Stew, 148
Kedgeree, 149
Tamarind Fish or Pudda, 149
Tamarind Fish, 150
Ballachong, 150
Prawn Ballachong, 151
Chilli Fry of Dried Bombay Ducks, 151
Tamarind Fry, 152
Jhal Fry, 152
To Pickle Beef, 153
Tholtee or Ding Ding, 153
Another way, 153
Mutton or Beef Stew, 154
Chicken Stew, 154
Pork Stew, 155
Indian Vegetable Stew, 156

BRINJALS
Brinjal Mussala Cutlets, 157
Brinjal Cutlets, 157
Brinjal Cutlets (Vegetarian), 158
Brinjal Cutlets (Meat), 158
Brinjal Cutlets (Fish, Prawn, Crab or Lobster), 158

Savoury Brinjal Cutlets (with or without Meat), 158
Brinjal Bake, 159
Fried Brinjal, 159
Fried Brinjals in Batter, 159
Brinjal Fry, 159
Rice Batter for Brinjals, 159
Behndi or Lady's Fingers, 160
Boiled Lady's Fingers, 160
Fried Lady's Fingers, 160
Minced Cutlets, 160
Chicken Cutlets, 160
Sheep and Lamb's Tongue Cutlets, 161
Brain Cutlets, 161
Potato Chops, 161
Prawn Cutlets, 162
    Another way, 162
Rice and Meat Cutlets, 163
Indian Stuffed Tomatoes, 163
Fresh Tomato Sauce for Cutlets, etc., 163
Tamarind Sauce, 164
Goanese Fish Sauce, 164
Vegetable Pickles, 164
Vinegar, 164
Indian Savoury Omelet, 165
Kofree Chillies – Sweet Pepper – Pepperoni, 165
Dried Chillies, 165
Devilled Nuts, 166
Boiled Drumsticks, 167
Kulee, 168
Kool, 168
Stewed Bombay Ducks, 168

SWEETMEATS AND SWEET DISHES
Jellabies, 169
Goolab Jamon, 170
Rasgollah, 170
Balashai, 170
Meeta Pillau, 171
Savia, 172

Chuckolee, 172
Madras Hulwa, 172
Pastry for Pustholes (Samoosas or Pooree), 173
Filling for Meeta Dhall Pustholes, 173
Filling for Meeta Naral Pustholes (Sweet Cocoanut Puffs), 174
Filling for Meeta Kayla Pustholes (Sweet Banana Puffs), 174
Filling for Meeta Anan-nas Pustholes (Sweet Pineapple Puffs), 174
Pineapple Balls, 174
Banana Fritters, 174
Pootoo Rice, 175
Thq-Thole, 175
Pootoo Rice Fritters, 175
Pootoo Rice Balls, 176
Rice Bread with Cocoanut, 176
Sweet Rice and Soojee Poorees, 176
Soojee Poorees, 176
Rice Balls, 177
Rice Pudding, 177
Rice Mould, 177
Raggie Mould, 177
Soojee Mould, 177
Rice Congee, 178
Rosa Cruickeese, 178
Beveca (Anglo-Indian), 178
Beveca (Southern Indian), 178
Beveca (Anglo-Indian and Southern Indian), 179
Beveca (Anglo-Indian and Deccan), 179
Soojee Kul Kuls, 179
Kul Kuls or Kajoors, 180
Panyarums, 180
Rice Flour Aliathrum, 180
Soojee Aliathrum, 181
Rogni Roti, 181
Indian Cream, 181
Kheer, 181
Cocoanut Sauce or Custard, 182
Koykotay, 182